Structured Play-Based Interventions for Engaging Children and Adolescents in Therapy

Angela M. Cavett, Ph.D., L.P., RPT-S
Child and Adolescent Psychologist
Registered Play Therapist-Supervisor

INFI∞ITY
PUBLISHING

Copyright © 2010 by Angela M. Cavett, Ph.D., L.P., RPT-S
Cover photo by Angela M. Cavett, Ph.D.
Back cover photo by Haney's Photography
Illustrations by Ella Cavett

From Head to Toe by Eric Carle, copyright ©1997 by Eric Carle.
Used with permission from the Eric Carle Studio.

Correspondence regarding Structured Play-Based Interventions for Engaging Children and Adolescents in Therapy can be sent to:
Angela M. Cavett, Ph.D
Email address: drcavett@yahoo.com
Website: www.childpsychologicalservices.com

ISBN 0-7414-6168-4

Printed in the United States of America

Published September 2010

INFINITY PUBLISHING
1094 New DeHaven Street, Suite 100
West Conshohocken, PA 19428-2713
Toll-free (877) BUY BOOK
Local Phone (610) 941-9999
Fax (610) 941-9959
Info@buybooksontheweb.com
www.buybooksontheweb.com

Dedication

This book is dedicated to my daughter, Ella, who makes each day playful.

And to the children, adolescents, and families who have given me the opportunity to accompany them on their therapeutic journeys.

Acknowledgments

First, I would like to thank the children, adolescents and families I have worked with in therapy. Accompanying others as they find the courage and hope to make changes in therapy is a gift. The work done in therapy is most beneficial when supported by a village of caring and committed professionals. Therefore, I want to thank the agencies in our area including Cass County Social Services, PATH, the Partnership Program through Southeast Human Service Center, and the Rape and Abuse Crisis Center.

I appreciate the support and guidance of several people in helping make this book come to fruition. These include Mrs. Jean Syverson, Kristin Garaas-Johnson, and Karla Buskirk who reviewed the manuscript and provided editorial assistance. Drs. Holly Hegstad and Jennifer Garaas were able to give clinical suggestions and guidance about whether interventions should be included. Most of all, I appreciate their friendship and peer consultation.

The Association for Play Therapy and several members of the association have been influential in my professional development and in the development of this book. I appreciate Bill Burns, CAE, Executive Director, and his mentoring of leadership classes to enhance members' governance skills and build relationships within APT.

Deb Butman-Perkins, NCC, LPC, QMHP, RPT-S, and Clark Perkins, NCC, LPC, from the South Dakota Association for Play Therapy have provided input and constructive advice during the development of this book and related presentations. I also appreciate their taking Ella to camp in the final week of revisions for this book. Their friendship, humor, and support are invaluable.

Liana Lowenstein, MSW, RSW, CPT-S has been a source of information on working with children, especially traumatized children. I believe her work, Paper Dolls and Paper Airplanes, is among the most important contributions to the field and have found new and innovative interventions in each of her publications. I appreciate the opportunities Liana gave me to initially offer the techniques I have created to other clinicians.

Sueann Kenney-Noziska, MSW, LISW, RPT-S, provided me the opportunity to learn about techniques that she developed and she encouraged me as I developed as a play therapist.

I appreciate all that I have learned from Athena Drewes, Psy.D., L.P., RPT-S through both her publications and the supervision I received from her. Dr. Drewes, the Director of Training for doctoral internships at the Astor Home for Children in Rhinebeck, New York, was instrumental in my training as an intern in 2001-2002, and allowed me to grow in many respects. I look forward to future collaboration with Athena.

David Crenshaw, Ph.D., ABPP, past Training Director at Astor Home for Children, was also influential in teaching me, mostly by showing me how to connect with children and colleagues in a respectful, loving, and accepting manner, allowing each individual to reach his or her full potential.

Table of Contents

Relaxation or Mindfulness   83

Interventions Related to Emotions, Thoughts, and Behaviors   91

Clinical Issues

Why use Play in Child and Adolescent Therapy?

In child psychotherapy, cognitive, social/emotional, and moral development guide treatment. Play, as the language of the child (Landreth, 1991) is developmentally appropriate in child treatment. Children use play to represent their experiences and views of self, others, and the world. Charles Schaefer has described the therapeutic factors of play (1999). Factors which are most relevant to the interventions in this book include: self-expression, direct and indirect teaching, stress inoculation, counterconditioning of negative affect, positive affect, sublimation, attachment and relationship enhancement, moral judgment, empathy, power/control, competence/self-control, sense of self, accelerated development, creative problem solving, and behavioral rehearsal, and rapport building.

Children use play to process concepts that they are not able to verbalize. Vygotsky (1967) found that children process in play at a higher level of cognitive development than what is consistent with their age (1967). Language, which is used in talk therapies, is less advanced than the child's nonverbal cognitions (Miller, 2002). Play in therapy allows for higher level processing of therapeutic issues.

How the Interventions were Developed:

Each of the techniques in this book was originally created to assist a specific child in learning a therapeutic concept that related to his or her treatment goals. As other children also presented with a need for the technique each of the techniques was modified to benefit a wider range of children. The goal in most of the interventions is to make an abstract concept more developmentally appropriate by making it concrete. The concepts which are typically words that the child does not fully comprehend are made more understandable. They are made concrete by performing relevant projects that the child can hear, see, and touch. For some interventions, the children can even taste or smell the concept. Projects are experienced and the process internalized. In all of the interventions, the children are able to manipulate the concept in a concrete manner which gives them mastery over an otherwise abstract concept.

Theoretical Orientation:

It is important for clinicians to understand psychological theories and have a theoretical framework from which to work. The interventions included in this book may be used across many theoretical orientations. They are most consistent with Cognitive Behavioral Play Therapy which is an integration of Cognitive-Behavioral theory and play (Knell, 1993). The interventions are directive, structured, experiential, and most importantly, playful.

Integrating Directive, Structured, Play Therapy Interventions and Handouts:

Children learn in many different ways. For most of the interventions, the playful hands-on activities will be the most beneficial. However, the child may benefit from additional opportunities and methods to process the concept. Therefore, with several of the interventions, handouts are included. The handouts also serve as transitional objects connecting the therapy to every-day life. They extend the benefits of the playful activity to allow the child to process it through a different modality, a written handout.

Clinical Judgment:

This book is intended for use by licensed clinicians or students in mental health fields who are under the supervision of a licensed clinician. The education and training of a mental health professional is necessary to make decisions about how the interventions may be used with a specific client. Children's mental health professionals are trained in assessment and evaluation, building a therapeutic relationship and using the relationship to make changes. This book and the play therapy interventions included are meant to be used within a therapeutic relationship to help clients move toward therapeutic goals.

The therapist must consider ethical obligations when using interventions. The ethical obligation for beneficence behooves the therapist to use interventions most developmentally appropriate. Playful interventions are typically the most developmentally appropriate approach to use with children. Another ethical consideration is non-malfeasance. At times a technique may not be appropriate for a specific child. Therefore, knowing the history of the client is important. For example, when abuse has occurred in the client's history, an intervention which may be engaging for one client may act as a trigger for a traumatized client.

Many interventions may have the potential to be helpful; however, depending on how and when the intervention is done it can be detrimental. For example, a child who has been photographed during child sexual abuse may be triggered if the Feelings Photo Shoot is done early in therapy and without adequate processing. If the client has done sufficient psychoeducation about sexual abuse, learned about feelings and the modulation of affect, discussed and processed the abuse and discussed their reactions to the abuse, the Feelings Photo Shoot may act as a powerful experience of in vivo exposure. Therefore the same intervention must be considered within the theoretical orientation of the therapist and within the applicable literature (i.e., abuse literature), as well as for the specific child, in order to assess appropriateness. Consideration of the child's presentation in the session is also important for intervention selection. Although a clinician may plan to use a specific intervention during a particular session, the therapist must be flexible in addressing other needs as they are presented and adjust the expectations of the session to fit the child's needs.

Advanced Preparation:

Clinicians are encouraged to do advanced preparation and practice the interventions prior to using any intervention with a client. This may include having the materials available as well as thinking through the intervention and whether its use would be appropriate for a specific client/patient. Often using an adaptation of the interventions (with the exception of those specifically for abuse issues) with non-clinical children can be helpful. Use of the interventions with children not involved in mental health services may give the clinician more information about how children may process the information and the differences in processing based on diagnosis.

Selection of Interventions:

Selection of interventions may be informed by observing the child. When sessions include at least a portion of nondirective play, the clinician has a view into the child's world. Charles Schaefer has described play as the language of the child (1995). Hearing and seeing the language of the child, including their interests and view of the world can be helpful when thinking about selection of directive interventions. It is not always possible to match an intervention with a known interest of the child's. However, looking for themes may guide the therapist in choosing appropriate interventions for an individual child. The themes of the child's discussions are heard when the child begins the session by discussing what extracurricular activities in which the child is involved. The assessment process can also be helpful in determining what interventions may be interesting and engaging for an individual child. A sentence completion completed by the child during the initial assessment will offer valuable information for later selection of interventions.

The interventions proposed by the play therapy community, including those of Liana Lowenstein, MSW, RSW, CPT-S; Paris Goodyear-Brown, MSSW, LCSW, RPT-S; and Sueann Kenney-Noziska, MSW, LISW, RPT-S, provide possibilities to address many therapeutic issues. As the clinician develops a toolbox of several possible interventions, he or she is able to choose from amongst those interventions, the one that is most likely to be helpful for an individual client. As the field progresses, clinicians will produce more interventions to address therapeutic issues by using different toys and props. Therefore, the likelihood of utilizing an intervention that will relate to individual children's interests and needs will be greater. The goal of this book is to contribute by offering additional unique interventions to treat children and adolescents.

Working with Parents:

When discussing interventions with parents, there are several important factors to communicate. First, parents often want to be assured that their child is making progress toward therapeutic goals. This is a valid position as they are concerned for their child and want to see them in less distress. Furthermore, parents invest time and money in the therapy process. At times, parents feel that using play in therapy means that the child is not benefiting from therapy but rather "just playing." Indeed, in practice I have had a parent tell me that he wanted his child to have "less play and more therapy." Of course, clinicians who use play understand the benefits of play, but some parents do not. It behooves us to spend time explaining, to the degree necessary for each parent, that the play is beneficial, if not essential, for therapy to be highly effective with children.

A second important issue to discuss with parents is that therapy is about the process, not the product. Often structured play/art therapy interventions result in a tangible item. The goal of the session is to create psychological change by decreasing symptoms and increasing coping skills. The product may also be helpful as it provides a transitional object and reminder of the therapeutic concept. The intervention used may result in a product, but the process is the crucial factor.

Third, parents and other caregivers are typically the child's most important advocates. A parent can be a co-therapist in the play therapy process within sessions. Following sessions, parents can assist and encourage children to use skills learned in therapy. By partnering with parents, the therapist is more effective in addressing the system in which the child is a part. Encouraging playful coping skills in the family is essential for meeting and sustaining treatment objectives.

Sections of this Book:

The interventions in this book have been categorized according to the phase of treatment. The initial section addresses assessment. Several interventions have been included to provide a variety of methods to collect information. Rock Paper Scissors, an assessment/rapport building game, is an assessment that can be utilized for varying lengths of time and across sessions. The Strength Genogram allows for the assessment of the child's perception of family members' strengths. The Adapted Puppet Sentence Completion Task provides sentence stems that elicit information about the child's view of self, others, and the world. Both the Strength Genogram and the Adapted Puppet Sentence Completion Task build upon the work of earlier play therapists to allow for further information to be processed. My Life Scavenger Hunt is a show-and-tell activity that allows the therapist to understand family dynamics while providing a view into the child's life. The information gathered with the assessments described in this book is beyond the typical scope of information that one can gather through standardized assessments. Used in conjunction with standardized tests, the clinician may have a deeper and broader understanding of the child or adolescent.

The Playful Treatment Planning section includes two treatment planning activities that allow for common metaphors for therapy to be used. The child is able to use the treatment planning as a time to express his or her views of presenting problems and hopes for therapy. The interventions also allow the therapist to describe what therapy is and provide a guide to the child that shows how the presenting problems can be addressed with interventions. Both treatment planning activities allow the child and family to visualize and verbalize their hopes for affective and behavioral change.

Several Feelings Identification and Modulation interventions are included in the following section. Most child and adolescent clients benefit from understanding their feelings. The interventions in this section allow for the therapist to address several affective issues. Understanding how feelings are shown by the child as well as others is addressed across most of the interventions. Measurement of the intensity of affect is addressed by Parachute Feelings Bounce-ometer, Abacus Feelings, Feelings Photo Shoot and Volcano of Anger. Emotional Memory and Feelings Photo Shoot promote understanding of the physiological reactions to feelings. Most also playfully teach coping skills for modulating anger.

Relaxation and Mindfulness interventions comprise the following section. The interventions provide playful methods of teaching relaxation to young children through adolescents. The Tighten and Relax Dance and Progressive Muscle Relaxation *From Head to Toe*: Game Playing to Shape PMR provide resistant young clients with games and play that promote learning the skills of relaxation. The Mindful Tasting intervention allows for a pleasant sensory experience that teaches about tolerating affect and mindfully experiencing and accepting situations.

Interventions related to emotions, thoughts, and behaviors include several interventions related to rational and irrational thoughts. These include I Shine, My View of the World, and Right Address/Wrong Address. The Magnetic Cognitive Triangle is an amazing tool for teaching about the cognitive triangle and assisting children and adolescents in expressing their feelings, thoughts, and behaviors as well as discussing triggers. Several other interventions address common problems including improving sleep, problem solving and assertiveness.

Interventions for Processing Trauma are processed with interventions from the next category. The first, Nested Boxes, allows the child a visual of the therapeutic process and specifically addresses how the child will be prepared for processing the trauma. It is empowering for the child or adolescent who has experienced trauma in that it provides information, sets healthy guidelines about when trauma will be processed and allows the child to better understand what skills need to be developed in order to better cope with the trauma history. Normalization of sexual responses in some children who have been sexually abused is addressed in the Pfffft That Just What Bodies Do. Jack-in-the-box is an intervention that provides a safe example of in vivo exposure to innocuous stimuli. The Quilt to Safety and The Spider and the Fly allow for processing of trauma and enhancing the child's safety.

The final section consists of four termination exercises. Three address building a supportive community to improve the child's opportunities for support and safety in the future. Light My Path, My Contacts and 411, and My Safe Neighborhood interventions provide the child with information about who is available to support them. The Light my Path intervention may also reinforce the supportive people in the child's team which may improve the likelihood that the child will be supported in the future. Putting the Puzzle Pieces of Resiliency Together is a termination intervention developed to help older children and adolescents consider their emotional condition prior to therapy and the gains made in therapy.

Language in the Book:

The use of "child", "adolescent", and "client" were used throughout the book. This was done with respect for the choice of words individual clinicians may use for the people whom they serve. For interventions most appropriate for younger children, the term "child" was used and those that are likely beneficial for older children and adolescents, "adolescent" was used. For interventions helpful across the range of children and adolescents, the term "client" was used. Furthermore, some clinicians may conceptualize the people they serve as consumers, patients, or clients. "Client" may be the most commonly used term to describe the typical child or adolescent with whom the play-based interventions are used. For consistency, "client" has been used throughout the book. Children are also referred to as both male and female throughout the book. It may be easier to read one pronoun; however, it seems important to include both male and female clients. In the intervention, Magnetic Cognitive Triangle, suggests are made of thoughts that may be written on magnets for the client to use.

For example, thoughts referring to child abuse, self blame, and disclosure refer to the perpetrator as male. Perpetrators may be either male or female, though statistically it is more likely that they are male. Therefore, to reduce redundancy, only the male pronoun is used. Furthermore, in clinical practice, where clients have used this intervention, almost always the pronoun used by the child was for male perpetrators. Many of the thoughts related to attachment have references to mothers which could also be similar to thoughts clients have about fathers. Again, to reduce redundancy, the more likely scenario has guided the suggestions.

Organization of Interventions:

Each intervention is organized related to the following sections:
- Title,
- Treatment Theme,
- Treatment Goals,
- Treatment Modalities,
- Materials,
- Cost of Intervention,
- Discussion, and
- Procedure.

The treatment themes include assessment and rapport building exercises helpful for understanding the client better and developing relationship. The treatment goals articulate the purpose of the intervention. The treatment modality includes individual, family or group therapy. Some interventions may be modified to fit a different modality than that which is stated. The Recommended Age Range is suggested for clinicians. However, interventions are often helpful for children outside of the range. For example, many can be used with much older children and even adults. The discussion section allows for theoretical information related to the intervention. Similar interventions are discussed, as well as how the intervention contributes to the current literature. The procedure is a step-by-step description of how to implement the intervention. Adaptations may be helpful with individual children and adolescents.

The Cost of Intervention is an assessment ranging from $ to $$$. Many interventions are in the inexpensive range. A photocopy-ready game is provided with Rock Paper Scissors. The Problem Solving Puzzle also may be photocopied from the book for use with children. The expense of the interventions utilizing art supplies depend upon the materials used. For example, puppets made from paper bags are very inexpensive and those made from blank puppets purchased from an art supply company, are also fairly inexpensive. Some interventions are in the moderate range of expense, which is symbolized by $$. Many of these interventions, such as Progressive Muscle Relaxation from Head to Toe: Game Playing to Shape which utilizes the Head to Toe Game by Eric Carle is a moderate expense (about $20) but can be used across unlimited sessions making the per use expense very low. The high range of expense for interventions is symbolized by $$$. These include those that are above thirty-five dollars. For the expensive interventions there is an initial expense but the materials have unlimited use.

Playful

Assessment

Title: Rock Paper Scissors

Treatment Theme: Assessment

Treatment Goals:
1. Develop rapport with the child.
2. Assess the child's view of self, others, and his or her world.
3. Increase communication with the use of a common game.

Treatment Modalities: Individual/Family/Group

Recommended Age Range: 4-18 years
(Cards chosen dependent upon client's age)

Advanced Preparation: Photocopy the questions on the pages that follow. If desired, use four different colors of paper or cardstock for the four question types. For example, the Rapport Building, School, Family and Friends questions may be copied to light green, light blue, pink and yellow, respectively. Cards may be marked with a 1 on the back for use by clients of all ages and a 2 for adolescents.

Materials:
Deck(s) of cards with quesions related to Rapport Building, School, Family, and Friends.

Cost of Intervention: $

Discussion:
This intervention is designed to take a simple game that children and families play and utilize it within the therapy session to develop rapport and engage the child in the process of sharing. The decks of therapy game cards focus on four content areas; Rapport Building, School, Family, and Friends. In the initial session, the rapport building deck may be selected. The therapist may also create client or diagnosis -specific decks that include questions related to the presenting problem and relevant coping skills. Benefits of this game are that it is both simple and inexpensive. It tends to be less threatening to the child than a formal therapeutic game since Rock Paper Scissors is commonly played. Another benefit is that the child and parent can use this adapted game in many settings (i.e., grocery store line, riding in the car) to connect abut their experiences. Families can create four questions that they may ask when they win the game and do not have the cards available. Parents may be assisted in creating additional questions as needed. Therapists can also utilize the game with other simple, common, and inexpensive games such as Tic-Tac-Toe.

Procedure:
The therapist asks the child whether he or she has played Rock Paper Scissors in the past and whether he or she wants to play it in the session. The therapist explains that instead of "pounding" the other's fist after winning a round, the winner can ask the other person a question. The therapist and child can continue for a defined number of cards or amount of time, or play as long as the child shows interest. This intervention can also be used during the first or last five minutes of sessions to engage in a fun activity that provides information about the child's thoughts, feelings, and experiences. All questions, especially closed-ended questions, may be followed up with additional questions as clinically indicated.

Rapport Building Cards

If you could be invisible for a day, what would you do?	What is your favorite food?
If you were stuck on an island for a week, and could take only one person, whom would you take?	If you could fly or have extraordinary strength, which would you choose?
What do you wish you were old enough to do?	What is your favorite color?
What do you miss most about being younger?	How are you different from others? How are you the same?

Rapport Building Cards

Do you follow trends of music or clothing?	On what show would you like to be a guest actor/actress? Who would you be?
Can you be independent and dependent?	Would you rather be a singer or a doctor when you grow up?
What does your bedroom look like?	Do you play it safe or are you an adventurer?
How do you celebrate your birthday? Do you usually have a birthday party?	Do you like to be casual or dress up? Do you treat people differently based on how they dress?

Rapport Building Cards

What lullabies do you know? Who taught them to you?	What are three words that describe you?
What is your favorite breakfast? Who makes it for you?	When you are sick who takes care of you? How do you find comfort?
A girl's parents do not recycle. She feels embarrassed by this. What might she do?	What do you think about adoption?
What helps you know whether you can trust your parents?	What is it like for kids whose parents have problems keeping their jobs?

Rapport Building Cards

What do you think of a girl who wears new clothing almost every day?	What jewelry do you wear?
Do you like amusement parks? What kinds of rides do you like and which do you not like?	What would you like as a nickname?
If you had an entire 24 hours to do whatever you wanted, with anyone you wanted, what would you do?	Has anyone played a practical joke on you? How did you feel?
What is your favorite movie? What do you like about it? Which characters do you identify with the most?	How do you show your feelings during movies?

Rapport Building Cards

What foods do you know how to prepare? For whom do you prepare them? How often?	What is your favorite music? Do your parents limit what you listen to?
Who is your best friend? What do you like about him or her?	In what ways are you creative?
Do you have a silly or sarcastic sense of humor?	Have you ever sung karaoke? How did you feel when doing it?
Do you have your own computer?	If you could be famous, what would you like to be famous for?

Rapport Building Cards

What is your favorite nursery rhyme? Who taught it to you? How old were you?	What meaning do you think dreams have?
What is your favorite possession? What makes it important to you? What would you do if you no longer had it?	If you could invent anything what would it be?
What is your favorite holiday? What does it mean to you? What do you do to celebrate it?	What is a saying from a book, movie, or song that you like?
Draw your greatest wish. How can you make it a reality?	What is your favorite joke? Do you tell jokes often?

Rapport Building Cards

Draw something you fear. What about it is scary to you?	Where is your safe place?
What was the most embarrassing thing that has happened to you?	Do others think you are happy when you are not?
What is the text message you like to receive the least?	Do text messages communicate what you want them to? Is it easier to be misunderstood when you text or talk?
How do others see you?	When do you stick up for others?

School Cards

What do teachers in your school do when they notice someone bullying others?	What is your favorite class?
Do you play sports?	Are you better at completing homework when you have a lot of time or when you are under pressure?
What do you do that you would be embarrassed about if classmates knew you did it?	How do you do in math? Do you enjoy math?
Are you considered more studious or athletic?	Should cell phones be allowed in school? Why? Why not? How do you feel about texting during class?

School Cards

What do teachers like about you? What do teachers wish were different about you?	Do you decorate your locker? Why? Why not? If so, how?
What things do you like in a teacher?	Do you have enough time to eat your lunch at school? How do you spend your lunch time?
What do you do if you do not understand something in a class?	What do you do during free time at school? Do you prefer free time or time when you are in class?
Do you have a band in school? Are you involved in it? What do you learn from playing an instrument?	What do you think your teachers do when they are not in school?

Family Cards

What are three words that describe your mother?	When do you feel closest to your father?
What are three words that describe your father?	When do you feel closest to your mother?
Has anyone in your family had a serious illness?	Have your parents ever gone on vacation without you? Where did they go?
How often do you see your cousins? Are they more like siblings, friends, or both?	How would you feel if a family member gave you and a sibling or cousin gifts? What if one gift was very expensive and the other cheap? What might be the reason for the difference?

Family Cards

If a teenager has a job should he or she help pay the family bills?	If an older child is misbehaving at what point should the parents call the police? What should the police do?
Are there words that you would not use around your parents that you use around your friends?	What do you think about a family who has a pet that they do not groom or feed well? Who should change the situation?
Who would you go to if you had a disagreement with your best friend?	Who has been your role model for relationships?
At what age do you think girls should date? Should boys begin dating at the same age?	How do your values differ from those of your parents? How do you feel about those differences?

Family Cards

At what age do you think teenagers should be allowed to drive?	What are your plans For your next vacation from school?
What do you wish your parents had taught you when you were younger?	How do you resist peer pressure?
When you were younger did your parents punish you? If so, how?	What time do you think is a reasonable curfew? Do your parents agree?
Do your parents like your best friend? Why?	How important is it to belong to a family?

Family Cards

What does your family do with toys when you have outgrown them?	What kind of music do you like?
What do you daydream about? Does daydreaming get in your way? Does it help you make goals?	Do you show off?
If you could spend all day reading or shopping, which one would you chose?	What type of dance do you like best?
What brand of clothing is most popular in your school? Do you wear it? Do different groups wear different brands?	What is your favorite book?

Friends Cards

A girl was texted by her best friend during class. What does she tell her?	What do you like to do with your friends?
Do you borrow clothing from friends? Do you lend clothing? Why?	If you needed 20 dollars for an emergency who would you ask for it? How do you feel about asking about this?
Who do you share your thoughts with when you are feeling down? Feeling excited? Is it the same person?	How is trust built? Do you trust others right away or over time?
Who do you go to for advice? What makes that person helpful?	What do you think when a friend becomes clingy?

Friends Cards

If you hear gossip, what do you do? What do you want to do? Is what you do and what you want to do the same? Why?	Do you gossip about others? What do you gossip about? What makes you want to gossip?
Do you like to be in charge or follow others?	Do you have friends who are girls? Boys? Why?
Which of your friends is the best listener?	What are three words that describe your best friend?
Who is your most loyal friend? What makes some friends loyal?	Do you have sleepovers? Who do you like to have over for sleepovers? Is it more fun to have planned activities for sleepovers or just go with the flow?

<u>**Title**</u>: Adapted-Puppet Sentence Completion Task

<u>**Treatment Theme**</u>: Assessment

<u>**Treatment Goals**</u>:
1. Establish rapport with the child.
2. Provide play as a means of communicating the child's experience.
3. Assess the child's self-report of feelings, thoughts, behaviors, and relationships.
4. Provide structure for the use of puppets in communicating in therapy.

<u>**Treatment Modalities**</u>: Individual

<u>**Recommended Age Range**</u>: 4-12 years
(Sentence stems selected based on developmental stage and presenting problems)

<u>**Materials**</u>:
Puppets (Available from Folkmanis)
Homemade puppets (Feelings Puppets Intervention)
Preschool and School-age Adapted Puppet Sentence Completion Tasks

<u>**Cost of Intervention**</u>: $ to $$$ depending upon cost puppets.

<u>**Puppet Selection**</u>:
The selection of puppets by the therapist for this intervention should represent a broad range of human emotions and behaviors. Irwin (2000) suggests using 15-20 puppets across a range of categories when using puppets to assess children. The following are examples of what may be represented in the puppet selection:
Human

- Range of ethnicity
- Range of professions (doctor, police officer, postal carrier, members of the military)
- Family members (Father, Mother, Boy, Girl, Baby, Grandparents, other human figures)
- Fictional/Fantasy human (princess, prince, Superman)

Animal

- Range of themes (Aggressive, Friendly, Happy, Sad)
- Predator
- Domestic
- Fictional animal (dragon)

<u>**Discussion**</u>:
The use of puppets in assessment and therapy has been referenced to since early in the history of child therapy. Both the Puppet Sentence Completion Task (PSCT) (Knell & Beck, 2000) and the Puppet Interview (Irwin, 2000) are excellent sources on the use of puppets in structured interventions with children for assessment and treatment. Eleanor Irwin introduced the Puppet Interview for children as an extension of the use of puppets in assessment and treatment of children (Irwin, 2000). The Puppet Sentence Completion Task (PSCT) was originally developed by Knell (1992). For a complete discussion of the original PSCT, see Knell and Beck (2000). This Adapted Puppet Sentence

Completion Task allows for additional sentence stems to be utilized by the clinician. The process incorporates procedural similarities to Irwin's Puppet Interview.

Sentence Completion tasks, which are projective measures, are commonly used with adults and adolescents for assessment. Initially, the literature suggested that children were not an appropriate population for the use of sentence completion tasks. However, Knell and Beck have suggested that this may be more a limitation of developmentally appropriate means of administering the sentence completion task than a true limit based on the developmental stage of the child (2000). Indeed, they developed the Puppet Sentence Completion Task (PSCT) that allowed this common assessment tool to be utilized with children in a developmentally appropriate manner. Knell suggests that children three years and older can respond to the original puppet sentence completion (1994). This is due to both the playful nature of using puppets as well as the verbal responses in lieu of written responses.

This Adapted-Puppet Sentence Completion Task, as with the original PSCT, is to be used along with other assessment tools including the clinical interview to gain understanding related to the child's history and behavioral observations. The following intervention allows for a rich view of the child's world through puppet play. It is a foundation from which the clinician can begin dialogue with the child. As with the original PSCT, the following fragments have not been standardized (Knell, 1994). Indeed, although they are helpful in understanding the child's view of self, others, and the world, they are also can be used therapeutically in addition to assisting with clinical assessment.

Knell and Cavett are currently revising the Puppet Sentence Completion Task. The revision will include specific stems for addressing several specific populations such as children with attachment issues, affective problems and behavioral concerns. Clinicians may also develop stems they find helpful in their practices or with a specific population.

Irwin, E.C. (2000). The use of a Puppet Interview to understand children. In: K.J. O'Connor & C.E. Schaefer (Eds.), *Handbook of Play Therapy: Volume 2 Advances and Innovations.* (pp. 682-703). New York: John Wiley & Sons, Inc.

Knell, S. M. (1993). *Cognitive-behavioral play therapy.* Northvale, NJ: Jason Aronson.

Knell, S. Cognitive-Behavioral Play Therapy (1994). In: K.J. O'Connor & C.E. Schaefer (Eds.), *Handbook of Play Therapy: Volume 2 Advances and Innovations.* (pp. 111-142). New York: John Wiley & Sons, Inc.

Knell, S.M. & Beck, K.W. (2000). The Puppet Sentence Completion Task. In: K.J. O'Connor & C.E. Schaefer (Eds.), *Handbook of Play Therapy: Volume 2 Advances and Innovations.* (pp. 704-721). New York: John Wiley & Sons, Inc.

Procedure:

The puppets are presented to the child by placing them within the child's reach. They may be in a basket or on puppet stands. If available, a puppet theater may be used. The therapist tells the child that he or she may choose to use the puppet theater or to act out the sentence completion without using the puppet theater. This decision is noted as the child may use the theater defensively for more emotional distance. An alternative explanation is that the child may choose the theater if they are more familiar with puppet theaters.

The child is offered the puppets and asked to select one. The therapist asks the child if he or she wants to select the puppets that the therapist is going to use. The child's selection of puppets is typically informative. When the child chooses a child puppet for self, the puppet chosen reflects a self portrayal of the child. When the child chooses a puppet from such categories as fantasy or animals, the choice is considered important information. For example, the child may choose a snake or a lion or a butterfly. As with Irwin's Puppet Interview, the child's puppet selection and interest in the activity as well as verbal and nonverbal communications are noted during the puppet selection. This information is integrated with other assessment and interview information.

Modeling is used to show the child what is expected. The therapist uses a puppet to start the first sentence fragment. The therapist's second puppet finishes the sentence fragment. The child may respond with a completion of the sentence stem. If not the therapist then uses the first puppet to start the sentence fragment again, pausing and looking towards the child. If the child does not finish the sentence, the therapist repeats the fragment with a suggestive inflection. Although typically the child responds by finishing the sentence fragment, at times the therapist may need to give instruction that the child's puppet can finish the fragment. After the child begins to complete the sentence stems, the therapist begins the sentence stems appropriate for the child's age either the Preschool or School-age Adapted Puppet Sentence Completion Task is utilized. At this time, the second puppet no longer finishes the sentence stems and it is removed. This eliminates the possibility of the child responding based on the therapist responses. It also allows the therapist hand to write the child's responses. As with the original PSCT, the fragments are answered utilizing the puppets, however if the child wants to answer them without using the puppet he or she may. (Knell, S. 1994, Knell & Beck 2000). The sentence stem pages may be photocopied for ease of use and completed statements are recorded.

Modeling completion of the sentence stems.

Puppet 1: Therapist
Puppet 2: Therapist
Puppet 3: Child

Puppet 1: My name is
Puppet 2: My name is (Common child's name from the client's culture)
Puppet 3: _____

Puppet 1: My favorite candy is
Puppet 2: My favorite candy is a sucker.
Puppet 3: _____

Puppet 1: At the park, I
Puppet 2: At the park, I swing.
Puppet 3: _____

Puppet 1: My favorite game is
Puppet 2: My favorite game is Candyland. (or other game the child may be familiar with playing)
Puppet 3: _____

Preschool Adapted-Puppet Sentence Completion Task

My mom_____ .

Time out is _____ .

Mom gets angry when _____ .

Kisses are like _____ .

Jumping is _____ .

Parents go to bed when _____ .

God may_____ .

Brushing teeth is _____ .

Hugs make me feel _____ .

Rules are _____ .

I feel safe when _____ .

Breaking a glass is _____ .

At the playground, I_____ .

My brother is afraid of_____ .

When it is cold outside, I_____ .

When I look out the window I _____ .

Hurting others means_____ .

When I am punished I _____ .

Seeing my parents makes me _____ .

The safest place in our house is _____ .

When I am big I would change _____ .

Drinking means _____ .

When a bird is hurt _____ .

Having a boyfriend/girlfriend _____ .

I often wish _____ .

When I was a baby I _____ .

I am afraid of _____ .

I admire _____ .

I think my mother _____ .

In our family, we _____ .

The worst time is when _____ .

I feel grossed out by _____ .

My father likes to _____ .

I don't want people to know _____ .

Having a pet means _____ .

My grandmother _____ .

Adoption is_____ .

I don't want to stop _____ .

On weekends I _____ .

My favorite movie is _____ .

When I am older I will_____ .

In the morning I _____ .

All I want is _____ .

When people hit_____ .

Police are _____ .

What I regret is _____ .

The best rewards are _____ .

Babysitters _____ .

School-age Adapted-Puppet Sentence Completion Task

My favorite subject _____.

Teachers are _____.

My mom_____.

When I get to school I want to_____.

When I do something wrong _____.

Mom gets angry when _____.

Kisses are like _____.

In our house, jumping is _____.

God may_____.

Brushing teeth is _____.

Hugs make me feel _____.

It is time for parents to go to bed when _____.

Rules are made in our family by _____.

I feel safe when _____.

Breaking a glass_____.

At the playground I _____.

My brother is afraid of_____.

When it is cold outside, I _____ .

Looking out the window makes me feel _____ .

Hurting others means _____ .

When I am punished I _____ .

Seeing my parents makes me _____ .

The safest place in our house is _____ .

My teachers would never guess _____ .

When I am big I would change _____ .

Drinking means _____ .

When a bird is hurt _____ .

Homework is _____ .

Having a boyfriend/girlfriend _____ .

I often wish _____ .

When I was little _____ .

I am afraid of _____ .

I admire _____ .

I think my mother _____ .

In our family _____ .

The worst time is when _____ .

On weekends I _____ .

I feel grossed out by_____ .

My father likes to_____ .

Before school each day _____ .

I don't want people to know _____ .

Having a pet means _____ .

My grandmother _____ .

Adoption is_____ .

I don't want to stop _____ .

My teacher feels that I _____ .

My favorite movie was _____ .

When I am older I will_____ .

All I want is _____ .

When people hit_____ .

Police are _____ .

What I regret is _____ .

Title: Strength Genogram

Treatment Theme: Assessment

Treatment Goals:
1. Allow for identification by the child with positive attributes of self and family members.
2. Broaden the view of family members to include both positive and negative attributes.
3. Encourage connection with relatives in their support system.

Treatment Modalities: Family/Individual

Recommended Age Range: 3-18 years
Process issues only as developmentally appropriate using clinical discretion.

Materials:
Large piece of paper or poster board
Pencil, pen, markers, crayons, markers
Either sand tray miniatures or
Magazines
Scissors
Tape

Cost of Intervention: $ to $$$ depending upon whether magazines or miniatures are used.

Discussion:
The Genogram is a powerful therapeutic tool to assess relationships among family members and familial patterns. For a thorough review of the Genogram see McGoldrick, M., Gerson, R., & Petry, S. (2008). Dr. Eliana Gil developed the Play Genogram as an extension of the genogram. With the Play Genogram, the child uses sand tray miniatures to depict his or her view of family members (Gil, 2006). Sand tray miniatures may be small human figures, animals, objects, and symbols. The Play Genogram allows the child to process feelings and thoughts about their family and the relationships between themselves and family members. For a full description of the Play Genogram see Gil, E. (2006).

Several extensions have been made to the original Play Gengoram. The Family Play Genogram includes the client and other family members (McGoldrick & Gil, 2008). Gil extended the Play Genogram to process cultural issues. Children use the miniatures to depict what their family members have taught them about their culture. Paris Goodyear-Brown had adapted the Play Genogram with the Preschool Play Geno-game (2002).

The Strength Genogram is an opportunity for a child to identify strengths of family members and connect with those strengths. This intervention, as with the original Play Genogram, allows for loosening of the restrictions that may be consistent with the client's culture (McGoldrick, Gerson, Petry, & Gil 2008). The miniaturizing of family members and relationships decreases restrictions against speaking about family problems (McGoldrick, Gerson, Petry, & Gil, 2008). It also allows the child to consider their perception or narrative of their lives and relationship patterns. The rigidity of family's verbal narratives often excludes some information. At times, the excluded information may include positive characteristics of family members. This extension of the Play Genogram was developed to address the exclusion of positive information from the personal and familial narrative.

Children often are responsive to their parents' spoken and unspoken rules. At times these rules relate to their view of others. This is often true with children of parents who are in conflict or when there is a history of abuse. It may result in rigidity in the child's personal and familial narrative which may be detrimental.

Parents in conflict, regardless of marital status, may have difficulty seeing positive aspects of the other parent. In divorcing families, when children feel loyal to one parent or another, they may feel restricted in expressing positive feelings about the other parent. The restrictions in expressing positive attributes may impact the child's view of self, especially if the child shares some characteristics with the other parent.

When a positive attribute could be either positive or negative depending upon how it is used, this may be difficult for the child. For example if a child is physically strong and aggressive, and that child shares those characteristics with a parent who was physically abusive, the child may reject that aspect of the self. Alternatively, the child may over-identify with an aggressive parent due to sharing some characteristics. The Strength Genogram may allow the child to accept a trait such as physical strength and discuss how he or she can embrace it and use it appropriately (i.e., athletic performance).

Clinical judgment must be used before, during, and after the Strength Genogram intervention if there is a history of child maltreatment. The child should be asked to think of positive characteristics only when the therapist has fully heard the child's experiences with different family members. If the therapist believes the child may feel that the intervention minimizes his or her experience, the intervention should not be done or should be processed before, during, and after to assess its appropriateness, effectiveness, the child's possible problem interpretations, and response to the intervention.

Despite the obvious need for caution, the Strength Genogram may be especially helpful for children who have experienced interpersonal trauma. In an abusive family the non-abusive parent may see the abusive parent as completely negative. This makes it difficult to discuss positive characteristics of the abusive parent and how those characteristics may have influenced the child. The positive characteristics are important in the child's therapeutic processing of the abuse. For example, the abusive parent's positive characteristics may have contributed to delayed reporting. At times a nonabusive parent will have difficulty understanding that although the abusive parent was abusive, there were likely also positive characteristics about that parent that the child enjoyed. A child may also benefit from identifying and processing the positive characteristics of an abusive parent as it allows for grieving the loss of those aspects which were positive.

Children from 3-18 years can benefit from the Strength Genogram. Cognitive and moral development is important to consider when using the Strength Genogram. Younger children tend to represent family members with concrete representations while older children may use abstract symbols to represent self and others (McGoldrick, Gerson, Petry, & Gil 2008). When considering strengths or "good" for children, it is important to consider their stage of moral development. At early stages of moral development, one is considered "good" depending upon the consequences (punishment and reward) they receive. Later the child's perception of "good" or "right" is based on whether the person follows rigid societal rules. As adolescents explore abstract thought, their moral development becomes more complex. Understanding how the child may view a person's strengths based on their stage of moral development is recommended. To allow the child to explore the strengths of significant people in their lives, the prompt "something that you like about them or something they are good at" is used.

Initially, it is often useful to create a Genogram early in the assessment phase which is accurate and based on parental report and review of clinical records. Later in treatment, if clinically indicated, the Strength Genogram may be done and the therapist may use the original Genogram to compare and contrast.

In the literature, there is support for either the therapist or the child leading the drawing of the Play Genogram. When the therapist draws the Genogram, the basic relationships are represented by placement consistent with the original Genogram. The Genogram includes immediate family, parents, and grandparents as well as any other important figures represented. Children often want to include child care providers, teachers, friends and pets. Accuracy is secondary to perception when the child draws the genogram. Ages and relationships for example are often not accurate but are useful clinical information for the therapist.

McGoldrick, M., Gerson, R., & Petry, S. (2008). *Genograms: Assessment and intervention.* New York: W.W. Norton & Company.

Gil, E. (2006). *Helping Abused and Traumatized Children: Integrating directive and nondirective approaches.* New York: Guilford Press.

McGoldrick, M., Gerson, R., Petry, S, & Gil, E. (2008). Family Play Genograms. In: M. McGoldrick, R. Gerson, & S. Petry (eds.), *Genograms: Assessment and intervention.* New York: W.W. Norton & Company.

Procedure:

The concept of the Genogram, a diagram of his or her family with the males represented with a square and the females represented by a circle, is described to the child. The child or the therapist may draw the Genogram depending upon clinical judgment. The Genogram is processed with the child as it is drawn on a piece of paper. The child is introduced to an array of toys or figures. Sand tray figures (human, animal, objects and symbols) work very well for this intervention. If the therapist does not have a diverse range of small toys for the task, magazines can be used to create a collage of the strength genogram.

The child is asked to pick a figure (or magazine picture) that represents each person's positive attributes or "something that you like about them or something they are good at." The miniature is placed on the paper where that person is represented with either a circle or square. The parent or therapist may help younger children with the placement of the figure. If using magazine pictures, the pictures are taped to the Strength Genogram. The child and parent discuss their choice of different figures for family members. The child, parent, and therapist process that a characteristic that could be positive can be either a strength or weakness. For example, someone who is energetic can use energy to create projects or may not be able to sit still in class. The child may want to represent another aspect of each or some of the family members. This is noted and the process is fluid as the child represents family members and self.

Pictures can be taken of the Strength Genogram. Often the pictures provide important insight especially if the task is done more than once during treatment. If clinically indicated, a copy of the picture can be sent with the child.

The following process questions may be used with adaptations for developmental stage of the child.

Process questions:

Tell me about which miniatures you chose to represent your strengths/mom's strengths/other family members' strengths.

Can you enjoy some things about a person but not others?

Do all your family members have some positive characteristics?

Who are you most like? Who are you least like?

Do you share some of the strengths your mother/father/grandmother has/had?

Would some of the negative characteristics that family members have be positive if used differently? Are there characteristics that a family member has that other family members also have but are used differently?

Who is most supportive of you? What characteristics does that person have? How are you similar to him/her?

If someone has hurt someone because of his or her negative behaviors related to a certain characteristic, can you still appreciate his or her strengths? Do you remember both the positive and the negative behaviors the person had with you?

What defines a person? Do his or her strengths make up for weaknesses?

A version of this intervention was previously published in: Cavett, A. M. (2010). Family strength genogram. In: Lowenstein, L. (Ed.), *Creative family therapy techniques: Play, art, and expressive activities to engage children in family sessions*. Toronto: Champion Press.

Title: My Life Scavenger Hunt

Treatment Theme: Assessment

Treatment Goals:
1. Build rapport with the child.
2. Develop an understanding of the child's life and home environment.
3. Assess the child's coping skills and resources available.

Treatment Modalities: Individual

Recommended Age Range: 4-18 years

Materials:
Scavenger list for child based on the developmental level of the child.

Cost of Intervention: $

Discussion:
The therapist gathers information from the child, parents, and referral sources. Predominately, the information is verbal or written and describes history and presenting problems. A view into the child's life is developed over time. The view may be enhanced by playfully engaging the child in the rapport building process with the My Life Scavenger Hunt. The My Life Scavenger Hunt allows for the child to present his or her life to the therapist by providing a "show-and-tell" activity. The playfulness of the intervention decreases resistance and allows the child to lead the process of getting to know him or her as a person. Furthermore, since scavenger hunts often include random items, the child and parent feel less defensive as it is seen as a fun activity, not an assessment. Therapeutically, My Life Scavenger Hunt allows the clinician to answer the following questions:

Does the child do therapeutic homework?

Does the parent engage in the homework?

Does the parent assist or direct the child? Is the interaction supportive? Does it facilitate sharing?

Does the child have access to reminders of his or her life story?

Does the child have a strong and positive support system and how accessible is it?

What interests does the child have?

How is the child nurtured? How are his or her basic needs met? By Whom? What does the child typically eat and who prepares it?

What opportunities does the child have available to him or her? How rich is the environment?

How child-friendly is the home? For example, are products such as shampoo made for children, i.e., tear-free? Do preteens have access to personal hygiene items?

Does the family have opportunities to enjoy each other and relax? If so, how and where?

What does the child do to relax and self soothe?

Procedure:

The therapist discusses the Scavenger Hunt with the parent explaining that it is a fun way for the child to share about him or herself. The therapist explains that he or she would like to have a view of the client's world and the client's perspective about it. Due to the nature of the intervention, with the child bringing items to the next session, the parents' permission for the child to do the scavenger hunt is requested. The parent is asked to consider participating in the scavenger hunt, especially with younger children, if this is deemed clinically appropriate. For older children and adolescents, the client may be told that they may include the parent. The dynamics of the parent-child relationship can be observed in the interactions related to the My Life Scavenger Hunt.

The child or adolescent is asked if they enjoy Scavenger Hunts. If the client has not gone on a scavenger hunt, the concept is explained. The developmentally appropriate list is given to the client. The therapist begins processing with the client what they might choose to bring for specific items. For example the therapist may say, "One thing on the scavenger hunt is a stuffed animal. Do you have a special one that you plan to bring?"

The client is encouraged to do the Scavenger Hunt and bring the items back for the next session. A specific way to bring the items may be discussed with the client and/or the parent. For families who use public transportation, the Scavenger Hunt may need to be adapted to only a few actual items and/or bringing photos of items in lieu of the item.

When the client returns, the therapist reflects on each item. The child is encouraged to discuss the items. If the client does not have an item, the therapist may choose to process the emotions related to this or may integrate it into the conception about the case that may be processed over treatment.

A version of this intervention was previously published in: Cavett, A. M. (2010). Our family life scavenger hunt. In: Lowenstein, L. (Ed.), *Creative family therapy techniques: Play, art, and expressive activities to engage children in family sessions.* Toronto: Champion Press.

Scavenger Hunt List for children aged 4-12 years

A children's menu or recipe used for a typical meal in your home

Something that helps you relax

Baby picture of the child with a parent

Baby picture of the child with another adult

Picture of someone important to you

Shampoo

Picture of your room (just as it typically is)

Stuffed animal

Pair of socks

Souvenir from a family trip

Something that you do when you are bored

Single serving snack

Something that represents your family's heritage or culture

Your favorite book

An item related to an extracurricular or church/synagogue/mosque activity

Favorite toy

4 things you want to use for "Show and Tell"

Scavenger Hunt List for Children aged 12-15 years

Recipe that the family often uses or a menu from a restaurant that is often used

Your baby picture with a parent

Your baby picture with another adult who has been involved with you throughout life

Picture of an important person

Shampoo

Picture of your room (as you would typically have it)

Pair of socks

Souvenir from a family trip

Corrected and returned homework

Something that helps you calm and relax.

Something you do when you feel bored.

Single serving snack

Something that represents your family's heritage or culture

Your favorite book

An item related to an extracurricular activity

Something used to communicate such as a cell phone or Facebook page

A program from a church/synagogue/mosque or extracurricular event

4 Things which are important to you

Playful

Treatment

Planning

Title: Caterpillar to Butterfly Treatment Plan

Treatment Theme: Treatment Planning

Treatment Goals:
1. Develop rapport with the child through structured play/art.
2. Encourage the child and parents to identify and articulate their treatment goals in a supportive manner.
3. Discuss the connection between the changes which are desired (treatment goals) and the techniques to address them (interventions).
4. Provide a concrete representation of the abstract concept of therapeutic change.
5. Encourage motivation throughout the treatment process by referring to the playful treatment plan.

Treatment Modalities: Individual/Family

Recommended Age Range:
> 4-10 years puppet show and art project
> 11-16 years art project or use of metaphor depending on the child

Materials:
Sheets of Art Foam or construction paper
Glue
Pipe cleaners
Glitter balls (Optional)
Tissue paper (Optional)
Stickers (Optional)
Paper
Markers or colored pencils
Caterpillar to Butterfly Puppet (Optional) (Available through Folkmanis)

Cost of Intervention: $$

Discussion:
In the intake session, the therapist discusses the child's presenting problems. This discussion typically begins with the parents as well as review of standardized testing. If assessments are utilized, the specific problem scores as well as the behaviors that they represent are discussed with the parents. Based on the presenting problems, goals for treatment are made clear with objective and measurable goals. This intervention extends the therapist and parent-based treatment plan to include the child's view.

Engaging the child in the therapeutic process is essential for successful treatment. A child may be more easily engaged in the treatment planning if this is done in a fun, creative manner. This activity involves discussing the concept of change in both an objective manner by stating treatment goals as well as using play and the metaphor of change. The problems and goals for this intervention should be focused on the child, his or her view of problems, and the child's desired outcomes.

The intervention can be modified related to age. For younger children, performing a puppet show and talking about change may be more helpful. It is best to assess the child's interest in active puppet play, verbal discussion, expressive arts or a combination of the different modes of communication. Preschool and early school-age children may enjoy the art project after a short puppet show. Older children and adolescents may benefit from doing the art project while they are talking about the metaphor of change.

Procedure:

The child, parent, and therapist discuss change and how a caterpillar makes a cocoon and changes into a butterfly. Clinical discretion is utilized to decide whether it is appropriate to include the parents in this activity. A simple story, like the following, can be used as well as a puppet such as the caterpillar to butterfly puppet by Folkmanis.

> **Once upon a time, there was a big, fuzzy, caterpillar that crawled slowly through branches. As he crawled he ate leaves to fill his tummy. He became very tired and felt the chill from the air. He wanted to snuggle up and stay warm while he took a long nap. He built a cocoon around himself and went to sleep. While he slept he dreamt of having beautiful, colorful wings that would catch the breeze and help him sail high into the sky. He dreamt about hanging out with other butterflies in a field of flowers. He wondered how he could change. He knew that he had within himself the ability to become all that he wanted to be. As he dreamt of changing, his body grew silky wings and his fuzzy round body lengthened. When he awoke he realized that he had changed from his caterpillar self into a butterfly. He needed to get out of his cocoon. He set his mind to getting through the difficult time and worked very hard to get beyond the cocoon. Finally he was free! He tried out his wings, awkwardly at first, but learned from watching the other butterflies how to catch the wind and where the brightest fields of flowers were. He had become what he had wished.**

The child is then told about therapy and how it is like a caterpillar making a cocoon and changing into a butterfly. For example, the therapist may state, "When you come to therapy there are things that you or your parents may want to change. These could be things like behaviors. (Briefly discuss some behaviors that the child's parents have noted. This discussion should be matter-of-fact and supportive of the child. It should communicate to the child that the therapist believes that the child can change the noted behaviors.) When we have behaviors that need to be changed, we can think of them as being like a caterpillar. When we think about changing, we can think of being in a cocoon. The caterpillar goes into the cocoon to change. Therapy helps us learn ways to change the caterpillar behaviors. The behaviors we want to have are butterfly behaviors. As we make changes in therapy, we can work toward having more and more butterfly behaviors."

The child and parent use art supplies such as foam, construction paper and pipe cleaners to create a caterpillar, cocoon and butterfly. The supplies used, and how to use them can be decided by each child. The patterns that follow may be used to trace or the child may make their own.

BUTTERFLY: The butterfly is cut from the construction paper or sheets of art foam. Foam, tissue paper, glitter balls, or stickers are used to decorate. See Figures 1, 2, and 5.

CATERPILLAR: The caterpillar may be created using two pipe cleaners twisted together and cut to the desired length. Alternatively, foam may be cut in the shape of a caterpillar. See Figures 1, 2, and 3.

COCOON: The child makes a foam or construction paper cocoon. See Figures 1, 2, and 4.

The parent and child list 3-5 feelings, thoughts, or behaviors which brought them to therapy. These are listed under the caterpillar and are discussed as the caterpillar behaviors. The goals for each respective problem area are listed under the butterfly and are discussed as butterfly behaviors. Interventions are written on the cocoon to address each of the presenting problems and the respective treatment goals. An intervention may address more than one presenting problem and treatment goal or several interventions may be listed for a single problem and treatment goal. Examples are provided below. Throughout treatment the caterpillar to butterfly treatment plan is referred to as they assess the behaviors of the past week and progress towards goals.

Caterpillar Stage:
Hitting sister when mad
Cocoon stage:
Learn ways to show anger that are acceptable (ex. I-Statements)
Butterfly stage:
Have less anger and express anger appropriately

Caterpillar stage:
Not listening to mom
Cocoon stage:
Use stickers to reward listening and use small reinforcements after four stickers are earned
Butterfly stage:
Listening to mom and following directions

Caterpillar stage:
Feeling sad or irritable
Cocoon stage:
Learn to talk about feelings including sadness in appropriate ways
Butterfly stage:
Have fewer sad moments and express sadness appropriately

Caterpillar

1. I hit my brother every day when I get mad.

2. I get too scared so I can't go to the bathroom without mom.

Cocoon

1 Learn to use words to express anger.

2. Learn ways to relax or distract myself when I am scared.

Butterfly

1 I will use words when I am mad.

2. I will be able to go to the bathroom by myself.
I will be less scared.

Figure 1: A completed Caterpillar to Butterfly treatment plan with the (presenting problems) caterpillar, (interventions) cocoon and (treatment goals) butterfly stages written by the child.

Figure 2: The Caterpillar to Butterfly Art Project created with art foam, glitter balls and pipe cleaners. Presenting Problems and Treatment Goals are compared to the caterpillar and butterfly as the child creates the art project.

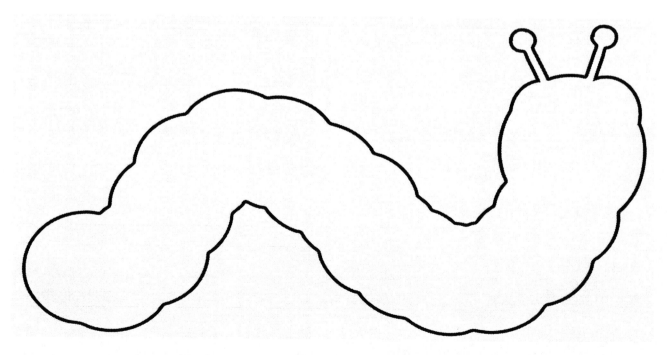

Figure 3: Template for caterpillar.

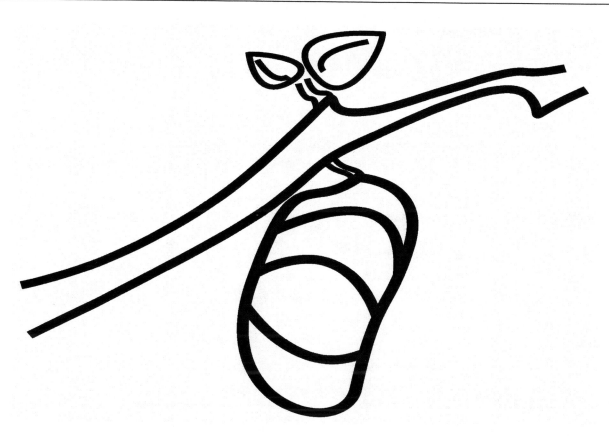

Figure 4: Template for cocoon.

Figure 5: Template for butterfly.

Title: Stepping Up to Success

Treatment Theme: Treatment Planning

Treatment Goals:
1. Engage the child in the treatment process and develop rapport by using a structured play-based intervention creating a visual that will be utilized throughout treatment.
2. Assist the child in discussing the connection between the treatment goals and the interventions.
3. Create a concrete depiction of the abstract concept of change.

Treatment Modalities: Individual/Family

Recommended Age Range: 4-18 years

Materials:
Construction paper
Glue
Markers, Crayons or Colored Pencils
Footprint template

Cost of Intervention: $

Discussion:
The treatment plan provides direction for the therapy for the therapist, parent, and child. Members of the treatment team may have different goals for the therapy. Discussion of each member's goals can create a more cohesive team. Using art and play at the beginning of therapy allows the child a natural means of communicating. In therapy, the metaphor of taking steps toward a goal is frequently referenced. This abstract concept is more easily understood by children by making the idea more concrete. This intervention was created after using Paris Goodyear-Brown's Step by Step intervention (2005). The current intervention does not provide the tactile sensation that the Step by Step intervention does; however, this intervention is easily referenced throughout treatment. The treatment plan can be referenced during each session for a moment at the beginning or end of the session to discuss how that session will be used to address the original problems. The original can be kept by the child, while a copy can be kept in the medical record. The art and play treatment plans are easier for the child to remember from session to session than verbal statements about presenting problems and progress towards goals.

In this intervention, the stair-steps represent the behavioral steps that need to be taken in therapy--the therapeutic goals. The footprints represent the specific interventions that can be utilized in and out of sessions to reach goals, or take therapeutic steps in session. The therapeutic goals are written on each step and the intervention is written on the footprint. For young children or those who are less comfortable with writing, drawings can be done for each step and intervention. Listing the interventions gives the child and parent some hope that they will learn coping skills that will directly address the problems which brought them to therapy.

Goodyear-Brown, P. (2005). *Digging for buried treasure 2: Another 52 Prop-based play therapy interventions for treating the problems of childhood*. Nashville: Paris Goodyear-Brown.

Procedure:

The parent and child are asked to think of the 3-8 main presenting problems and treatment goals on which they want to focus. The child and parent are asked to make stair-steps from construction paper or foam which will represent the problems that they want to address. The templates that follow may be used or the child may draw their own. Treatment goals for each of the presenting problems or the interventions that will be utilized to meet the goals are written on the stair-steps. The steps are glued on a piece of construction paper. The child may dictate the goal or may write it him or herself. For example, a treatment goal may be "to worry less." The child, parent, and therapist discuss how the goals can be met. For example, if a treatment goal is to reduce anxiety, an intervention to meet that goal may be to learn progressive muscle relaxation. The child or parent-child dyad makes footprint cut-outs with construction paper. The child then places a footprint on each of the steps. The child and therapist discuss how the steps represent the problems and goals to be addressed in therapy. The footprints represent the coping skills the child needs to develop in therapy to meet the respective goals. The Steps to Success treatment plan is photocopied and a copy is sent home to remind the child and family of the goals and coping skills. The original is reviewed at sessions to guide the treatment and encourage the child to build coping skills. Celebrate during sessions as the coping skills outlined on the footprints are developed.

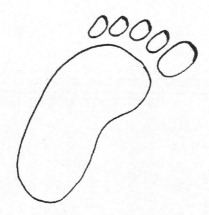

Figure 1: Footprint for writing the child's coping skills or interventions that will be used to address the presenting problems.

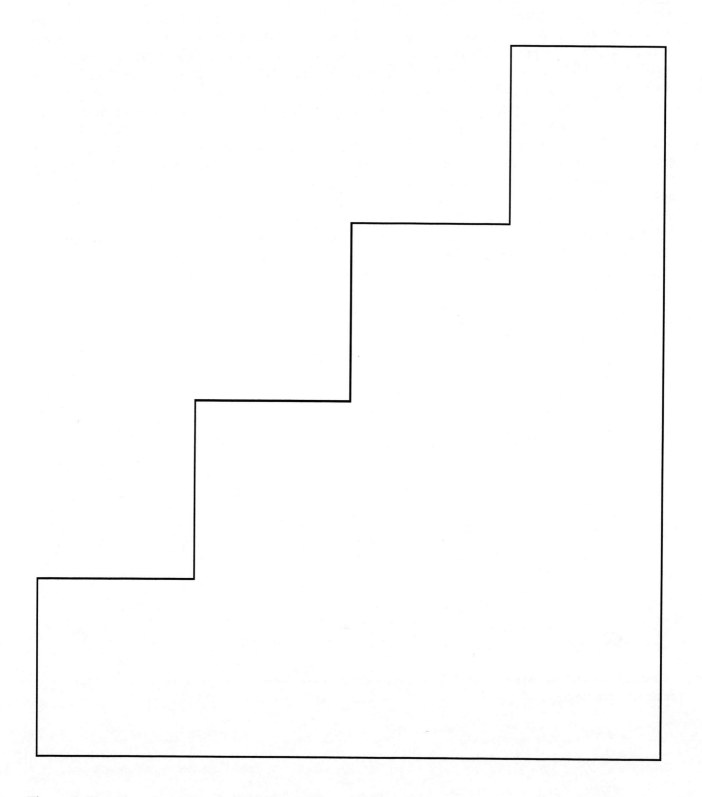

Figure 2: Template for steps on which the child and parent write the presenting problems.

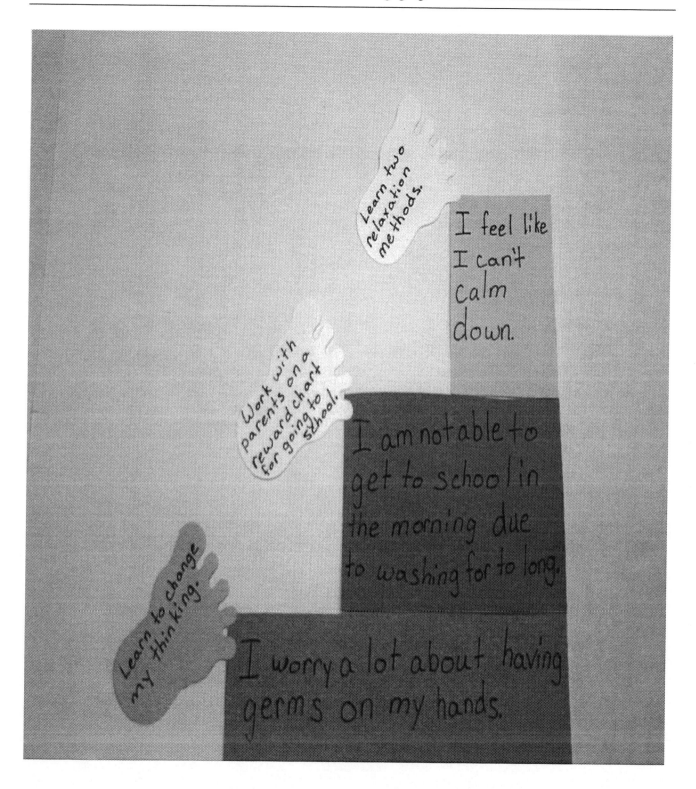

Figure 3: Several presenting problems related to anxiety are written on the steps, and interventions that will be utilized to address the presenting problems are written on the footprints.

Feelings

Identification

and

Modulation

Title: Feelings Puppets

Treatment Theme: Feelings Identification and Modulation

Treatment Goals:
1. Establish rapport with the child through play.
2. Provide play as a means of communicating the child's experience.
3. Assess the child's self-report and understanding of feelings.

Treatment Modalities: Individual

Recommended Age Range: 3-12 years

Materials:
Puppets ready to design (Available from Discount School Supplies)
Paper bags: lunch size
Markers, crayons, colored pencils
Decorations for puppets: Feathers, cloth, buttons

Cost of Intervention: $

Discussion:
This is an inexpensive and simple intervention with great clinical utility. Puppets are a valuable resource for child psychotherapy. They allow distance from direct discussion and reduce resistance. Puppets are typically expensive and to provide a varied array, it is a substantial investment. Making one's own puppets and allowing children to make several of their own can be inexpensive and provide an additional intervention related to feelings identification and expression. When the child is allowed to create their own puppet, the child is able to communicate individual feelings and discuss how different facial expressions are associated with feelings.

Procedure:
Paper bags (or cloth puppets such as those available through Discount School Supplies) and art materials including colored pencils, markers, and crayons are offered to the child. The child decorates the puppets with the art materials of his or her choosing. Buttons, feathers, and beads can all be used. The therapist and child list feelings. This can be most helpful when at least happy, sad, angry and scared are represented. Puppets can be made to represent each of the feelings. Puppets of each of the child's family members may also be created. The feelings represented on the child and his or her family members are noted.

Figures 1 and 2: A puppet made from a paper bag.

Figures 3 and 4: Puppets drawn by a child. Inexpensive puppets on which children can draw are available from Discount School Supplies.

Title: Anger Menu/Coping Skills Menu

Treatment Theme: Feelings Identification and Modulation

Treatment Modality: Individual/Family/Group

Recommended Age Range: 3 years to 16 years (Modified for developmental stage)

Treatment Goals:
1. List at least eight ways to express anger.
2. Discuss and problem solve about which may be appropriate ways to express anger.
3. Assess family dynamics and unwritten rules that may impede appropriate expression of anger.
4. Reduce unacceptable expressions of anger and replace them with appropriate ways of expressing anger.

Materials:
Menus from several local restaurants including those children enjoy
Paper
Pencil

Cost of Intervention: $

Advance Preparation: Ask local restaurants for children's menus

Discussion:
Learning about feelings, including anger, is an important goal of therapy. This intervention is an engaging activity that allows for discussion of behavioral options related to anger. The distance allowed by discussing one's favorite restaurant allows the child to playfully discuss options. This intervention also provides opportunity to talk about familial attitudes about anger and how their family expresses anger.

Procedure:
Start a conversation about the child's favorite restaurant and entree. Discussion continues revealing whether he or she has ever tried any other meals at that restaurant and the options he or she has when he or she goes to that particular restaurant. For example, the child and therapist discuss how some days one feels like having chicken nuggets and other days a hamburger. Different people like/prefer different things; for example, parents select different menu items than their children. Beverages, appetizers, and desserts are all mentioned so that the child gets the idea that many options are available and a menu is used to communicate what options are available. A menu is a nice way to display options and different people may choose different ways to express anger and different times or under circumstances an individual person may choose different ways to express his or her anger.

Anger Menu is written at the top of a blank sheet. The child lists ways he or she can express anger. The number of options may vary depending upon age. The Anger Menu is folded into quarters and in each quarter, methods of expressing anger are written on the menu. At least two pages, with four interventions on each page, are used. Beside each intervention, the child draws him- or herself engaged in that method of expression. Several pages may be used with four per page and pictures (visual cues) with each.

After the child has constructed the Anger Menu, the child and therapist talk to the child's parents about the importance of expressing anger. Some parents are fearful and do not accept certain expressions of anger. The menu allows for open discussion on accepting the feeling of anger, even if the expression of anger is not acceptable. With the therapist's guidance the parents may explore the child's necessity of expressing anger and needing permission to express it in an acceptable manner. Discuss parents' own expression of anger and the discrepancies between what they do and what they expect the child to do. If there are discrepancies, they are discussed.

This activity can also be used to create Coping Skills Menus for children with both internalizing and externalizing disorders. List eight or more coping skills. Be sure to include a variety of coping skills such as those that include auditory, tactile, visual and cognitive skills. Examples may include: listening to music, wrapping up in a blanket, talking to a friend, petting a kitten, helping others, 4-square breathing, Progressive Muscle Relaxation, listening to a relaxation CD or reading a book such as *A Boy and a Bear* by Lori Lite. Then construct a coping skills menu with four options listed per page, complete with drawings of each coping skill description. Both the Anger Menu and the Coping Skills Menu can be displayed in the home (i.e., on the fridge) to be consulted when the child needs to find a way to express anger or needs to pick a coping skill. The coping skills may be those practiced in previous sessions. If the child has few acceptable options, new coping skills can be suggested by the therapist and taught and practiced in future sessions.

Figure 1: An Anger Menu drawn by a child. The options are drawn by the child for a visual reminder.

Figure 2: Anger Menu drawn by a child.

A version of this intervention previously published in: Cavett, A.M. (2010). Anger Menu. In: Lowenstein, L. (Ed.) *Assessment and treatment activities for children, adolescents, and families. Volume 2: Practitioners share their most effective techniques.* Toronto: Champion Press.

Title: Feelings Memory and Feelings Memory Times Three

Treatment Theme: Feelings Identification and Modulation

Treatment Goals:
1. Assess the child's ability to identify feelings in self and others.
2. Provide psychoeducation related to feelings expression, physiology, and typical situations related to the feelings.

Treatment Modalities: Individual

Recommended Age Range: 6-12 years

Materials:
Feelings and Physiology cards
Cards depicting people showing different emotions that correspond to those in decks 1 and 2 (Optional for Feelings Memory Times Three) (Available at Childswork Childsplay)

Cost of Intervention: $

Advanced Preparation:
Two sets of cards are included on the pages that follow. The first set of cards has a feeling word on them. The second set gives a brief description of the physiological reaction common to a feeling as well as a time someone may experience that feeling. Prepare the cards by cutting them out and laminate if desired.

Discussion:
Children in therapy benefit from learning about feelings. This includes the range and intensity of feelings. Common scenarios related to different feelings can help children understand feelings in themselves and others. The physiological responses common to different feelings are also important. Often the physiological responses to feelings are taught with discussion or handouts. However, this intervention makes the concepts more playful. It also includes both auditory (discussion of feelings and physiology) and visual stimuli related to the task.

Procedure:
The child and therapist place the cards upside down. The therapist explains that with the original Memory game, you match two cards with the exact same picture, with Feelings Memory, the cards have a feelings word on half and a description of the corresponding physiology associated with the feeling on the second half. When the player flips a feelings word and the corresponding physiology, the player wins that "match" and keeps the cards in his or her pile. For example, when a player flips Angry and the physiology card that indicates fast heart beat, tight muscle tone, and frown, as well as the scenario of "when a bully repeatedly kicks me" that player has a match.

It may be helpful to review the cards and their matches prior to playing to introduce the concepts of physiological responses associated with different feelings. When introducing the feelings and throughout the game, the therapist discusses typical responses to feelings and how some people may not respond the same. For example, some people may not always smile when they are happy or frown when they are sad.

Feelings Memory Times Three:

A modification to the game may be played using a third set of cards. This modification is called Feelings Memory Times Three. The third set of cards (which are not included in the book) is different from the other two decks, both on the front and back. The third set would be either homemade or commercial cards of people expressing emotions that match decks one and two. Decks of cards depicting different feelings can be made by taking digital pictures of the child (with parent/guardian/custodian's permission) or having the parent take pictures of the child depicting the feelings. Alternatively, the therapist can use a commercial deck of cards such as those from Childswork Childsplay. The player turns turn over three cards one of which is a picture of a person showing an emotion. If all three cards: the name of the feeling, the physiological response and the picture of the feeling; match, the cards are won. This can raise the level of complexity and be more challenging for older children.

Name of activity: Parachute Feelings Bounce-ometer

Treatment Theme: Feelings Identification and Modulation

Recommended Age Range: 3 to 16 years (Adapted to the child)

Treatment Modality: Family/Group

Goals:
1. Provide psychoeducation about feelings identification in self and others.
2. Introduce the concept of intensity of feelings.
3. Provide a visual-motor intervention for expression of affect.

Materials:
Small Parachute (Available through Oriental Trading)
Small plastic air-filled balls

Cost of Intervention: $$

Discussion:
A common goal of therapy is to understand feelings beginning with identifying feelings in self and others. After the child has an understanding of identifying feelings, understanding the concept of the intensity of an emotion is helpful. Measuring the intensity is a more advanced concept. Children often have difficulty identifying feelings until they are felt "a lot" or "a whole bunch." This intervention promotes learning how to express the range of intensity of affect. Sitting still to look at a "Feelings Thermometer" may not be very exciting to some children. For some, a verbal discussion such as a rating scale (0-10) may be boring. The physical aspect of this intervention engages children who are more active, tactile learners who need to learn about feelings and intensity thereof through movement. Having a measurement that allows for expression with physical movement allows the child to show intensity of affect while at the same time learning to verbalize the concept.

Procedure:
The children and therapist may begin by playing with a colorful parachute. They may lift and lower it and go under it. The balls may be introduced and the children and therapist experiment with placing one or more balls onto the parachute and shaking it lightly, moderately, or hard. The therapist gives examples of scenarios that are related to a feeling such as happiness and these are discussed during the play. Scenarios that relate to different levels of intensity of affect are used. For example, scenarios may depict "a little" happiness, a "moderate" amount of happiness, and "a lot" of happiness. The balls are individually placed onto the parachute and the therapist tells about a scenario. The child raises and lowers the parachute bouncing the balls according to how much happiness they would feel if they experienced the scenario. The "a little" scenario may be: "My grandma gave me a piece of candy." The parachute is raised and lowered slowly. The "moderate" happiness may be: "I get to ride bike with my friend." The parachute is raised and lowered a medium amount. The high scenario may be: "Going to an amusement park" and the parachute is quickly raised and lowered with the balls flying up and down and off. The therapist asks each child to tell of a time that he or she felt a certain feeling and then shake the parachute to represent the intensity of the feeling at that time. A range of feelings are discussed. At times, to keep children engaged it is helpful to allow for additional play such as going under the parachute or putting several balls on the parachute and bouncing them.

Title: Feelings Photo Shoot

Treatment Theme: Feelings Identification and Modulation

Treatment Goals:
1. Assess the child's verbal descriptions about feelings and the intensity of feelings.
2. Increase the child's ability to identify feelings in self and others.
3. Assist the child in better understanding physiological responses and common situations related to feelings and behavioral responses.
4. Increase acceptance of the child's feelings and increase responsibility for appropriate behavioral responses to feelings.

Treatment Modalities: Individual/Family/Group

Recommended Age Range: 3-18 years

Materials:
Digital Camera
Paper
Pencil/crayons/markers
Large scrapbook (Optional)
Feelings Photo Shoot Handout

Cost of Intervention: $$$ (Depending upon cost of photo printing)

Discussion:
Feelings identification in self and others is considered one of the essential goals for many children in therapy. Therapists often have commercial pictures of people with different facial expressions displayed on posters or hand-outs. The pictures may be of real children or cartoonish characters. It is beneficial to have pictures of children with feelings that are realistic. Another benefit to commercial feelings products is that the child can see a variety of ethnic backgrounds, ages, and genders. Cartoon characters can also be beneficial in that they allow the specific facial features that are typical for that emotion to be emphasized. For example, when angry, one's eye brows can be furrowed and eyes squinted, while one's mouth is in a tight frown.

Despite the noted benefits, commercial products (whether they are of people or cartoons) present some limitations. Most importantly, the child does not see the people with whom he or she has the most contact. A child's mother may express anger a bit differently than the models in a feelings poster. Another related limitation is that feelings posters rarely show the subtle expression of feelings that is most commonly presented in daily life. A child may come into contact with others expressing fear with wide eyes and opened mouth on occasion but more often will see in themselves and others subtle expressions such as worry that may include eyes looking off, a tight mouth, or slight frown.

When pictures are taken, children can use the pictures in therapy. They may also take them home for use in understanding feelings in the family. This allows for greater generalization of the concepts.

The Feelings Photo Shoot can be helpful for the entire family and can allow the child to have a record of what certain family members look like when they have certain feelings. The Feelings Photo Shoot with multiple family members allows the child to play the roles of photographer and model at different times. Close friends or school personnel can also be photographed if this is considered beneficial. This can be especially helpful with children on the autistic spectrum or those with severe attentional deficits who may have difficulty with the subtle differences between individuals with the same feeling.

Children who have experienced or may have experienced being photographed during sexual exploitation/abuse should not be presented with this intervention without considerable clinical consideration. It may act as a trauma cue if done too soon, before coping skills can be developed or without empowering the child first. If done appropriately, after processing the child's trauma and as an exposure to the innocuous stimuli of being photographed in a nonabusive manner, it may be beneficial. Parental or custodial consent and understanding of the intervention with this population is essential.

Procedure:

The child is asked to list several feelings and the feelings, which are written either by the child or therapist. The therapist can add feelings after the child has exhausted his or her list. Each feeling is briefly discussed with the processing questions that follow. A book of 5 or more feelings is created. Older children and adolescents may benefit from an extensive list of 20 or more feelings. Feelings across a continuum such as anger are discussed. The template that follows can be used to create the portfolio of feelings from the Photo Shoot. This activity can also be done at home if clinically indicated (dependent to a great extent on the ability of parents to be supportive and helpful to the child during the activity). Whether the pictures are taken at home or the office, it is important to review the pictures and responses in therapy.

The Feelings Photo Shoot handouts that follow may be used or the child may create his or her own. Important factors related to the feeling are discussed with the child and documented on the handout on which the photo is adhered. The handouts that follow explore several issues which are outlined on the handout; however, if the child creates his or her own pages the therapist may offer guidance regarding exploration of these issues. The child is encouraged to explore the feeling including physiological reactions and times when he or she has felt it. Exploration of thoughts is also discussed. The child's typical behaviors when he or she has the feeling are also explored. The handout may be marked with X's to symbolize the child's response.

Processing Questions:

What do you look like when you feel _____?

What does your mom/dad look like when they feel _____?

Do your friends show _____ differently than you or your parents or brothers or sister? If so, how do they show it?

What does _____ feel like in your body?

What are some things you typically do when you feel _____?

What are some things that you think may be a better way to show _____?

Feelings Photo Shoot

Feeling: _____

Draw or attach picture of the child
expressing the feeling here.

Body Responses to the Feeling:

Heart beat: Slow	Normal	Fast
Breathing: Slow	Normal	Fast
Muscle tension:	Tight	Relaxed
Other bodily sensations:		

Times I usually feel _____.
1.
2.
3.
4.

Things I think to myself when I feel _____.
1.
2.
3.
4.

Behaviors: Things I might do when I feel _____.

1.
2.
3.
4.

Feelings Photo Shoot: Example

Feeling: Angry

Body Responses to the Feeling:

Heart beat: Slow	Normal	Fast X
Breathing: Slow	Normal	Fast X
Muscle tension:	Tense X	Relaxed

Other bodily sensations:

Times I usually feel __ANGRY_____.
1. When my parents argue.
2. When my friends do not call.
3. When I have to do homework.
4.

Things I think to myself when I feel _____ANGRY_____.
1. This is not fair.
2. Things will get better.
3. If I work hard, I will get this done and be able to play.
4.

Behaviors: Things I might do when I feel _____ANGRY_____.
1. Yell
2. Go to my room
3. Call a friend
4.

Title: Abacus Feelings

Treatment Theme: Feelings Identification and Modulation

Treatment Goals:
1. Assess the child's ability to identify feelings and the intensity thereof in self and others.
2. Assist the child in communicating feelings intensity using a concrete representation (abacus beads) for intensity.
3. Increase acceptance of the child's feelings and increase responsibility for behaviors related to feelings.

Treatment Modalities: Individual

Recommended Age Range: 4-16 years

Materials:
Abacus (Available through Melissa and Doug Toys)
Feelings list on cardstock
Magnets
Round Magnets and Magnetic Tape Strips with foam adhesive (Optional)
Hot glue gun and stick
Feelings pictures (Optional)

Cost of Intervention: $$

Advanced Preparation:
An abacus is prepared by gluing, with a hot glue gun, a magnet on the frame to the right of each row of beads. Alternatively, magnetic tape strips can be used. See Figure 1. Cardstock is cut into small pieces ensuring the magnets are able to hold them to the abacus. Each piece has a feeling written on it. See Figure 2. Several feelings should be represented. On the back of each cardstock piece, a magnet is fastened with hot glue. Alternatively, round adhesive magnets can be used. The child then selects the feelings on cardstock and fastens them to the abacus. A broad range of feelings can be available to use with the abacus. See Figure 3. Blank cardstock rectangles can be available with magnets attached for the child to add additional feelings as needed.

Discussion:
Feelings identification is foundational for effective therapy. After identifying feelings it is important to have ways for a child to express the intensity of the feeling. Often children are able to identify that they are mad or sad only after reaching an intensity that is moderate or high. For example, children may describe realizing that they are angry only when they are starting to yell at or hit their sibling.

Several means of expression of feelings intensity have been suggested in the literature. Canino and Spurlock have suggested communicating intensity of affect by using soft to loud sounds for children who are auditory learners and communicators (1994). For those who are visual, one can use colors (Canino & Spurlock, 1994). As the intensity of the feeling increases the child can make the color darker. For example "a little bit sad" is light pink; "a medium amount" of sadness is medium pink and "a lot sad" is darker pink. Goodyear-Brown (2005) created an engaging activity, Mad Maracas, which allows the child to process intensity of feelings by shaking maracas with varying intensity. The Feeling

Bounce-ometer, described in this book, is an option for an active expression of feelings intensity. Any of these interventions are recommended at an early stage of therapy to provide more understanding of feelings intensity to the child or adolescent.

This intervention was developed as a simple and quick intervention that can be easily used across sessions. It is offered as an alternative to the Feelings Thermometer. Even young children seen in therapy a decade ago had an understanding of the thermometer. When they were ill, their caregivers would use a mercury thermometer to take their temperature. As their temperatures went up, the mercury went up. Now fewer children have experience with mercury thermometers every year. With digital thermometers being used more frequently, the thermometer as a simple tool to easily explain feelings intensity and measurement has become out-dated.

A benefit of the Feelings Abacus is that it is easy to use for both in-depth discussions during the initial discussion about measuring the intensity of feelings, and it also can be a very brief intervention used in sessions following the initial presentation of the concept. It is also helpful to have the measuring units contained, as they are with an abacus. This reduces the time spent taking out and putting back small pieces that can be used to represent feelings intensity.

Procedure:
The child or adolescent discuss the range of feelings he or she is familiar with. Each of the feelings is discussed along with how the feeling feels in the body, and what the client typically does when he or she has that feeling. The client and therapist talk about intensity of feelings. The abacus is presented and different scenarios are discussed with the client and therapist discussing how much of a feeling may be associated with the scenario. The child moves the corresponding amount of beads to represent the amount of the feeling.

After it has been initially introduced, the abacus may be used briefly during sessions to discuss present mood, his or her mood over the past week, or related to issues discussed in the session. If processing trauma, the child may use the Abacus Feelings intervention while discussing the child's life history or a trauma narrative.

Figures 1 and 2: The abacus with a magnetic strip adhered along the right side. The magnetic strip with feelings attached to it. The feelings are chosen by the child with the intensity represented by the number of beads moved to the right side.

Figure 3: The Feelings Abacus with several feelings attached to the magnetic strip. Intensity is represented by the number of beads moved to the left.

<u>**Title**</u>: Volcano of Anger

<u>**Treatment Theme**</u>: Feelings Identification and Modulation

<u>**Treatment Goals**</u>:
1. Use a concrete representation of the abstract concept of anger expression.
2. Increase the child's understanding of intensity of anger across a continuum.
3. Increase ability to think about appropriate expression of anger and modulation of anger.

<u>**Treatment Modalities**</u>: Individual

<u>**Recommended Age Range**</u>: 4-12 years

<u>**Materials**</u>:
Volcano Model (Erupting Cross Section Volcano available through Learning Resources)
Baking soda
Vinegar
Red food coloring
Dish soap
Post-it notes
Shirts that can protect clothing
Plastic sheet such as a shower curtain or old newspapers
Volcano handout

<u>**Cost of Intervention**</u>: $$$

<u>**Discussion**</u>:
Often angry and aggressive children are told that their anger is like a volcano erupting. The metaphor of erupting is helpful for many children to visualize. The metaphor is commonly used; however, most children have little experience with volcanoes and the abstract concept of being like a volcano may be better processed experientially. This intervention allows the child to experience an eruption.

The analogy of the child being like a volcano when he or she is mad allows for discussion about levels or intensity of anger. As anger increases, the likelihood of erupting does as well. Thoughts about the situation and using coping skills are important factors in whether the situation is responded to with an eruption or a more appropriate expression of anger. This intervention allows the child to learn about the levels of intensity of anger. A volcano model that opens to allow for the teaching of the layers is helpful for teaching about the intensity of anger.

As with other interventions, the more tangible the intervention tools, the more likely the child will be engaged in the process, will learn the concept, and integrate it into their lives. Although anger can be discussed with handouts or just a verbal discussion about anger erupting, it comes to life with this intervention. This intervention may be done without a model or with a model that does not open; however, it may be worth considering acquiring a model to make it more "real."

Cleaning up after the volcano eruption can also provide an opportunity to talk about the fallout of emotional eruptions. If contained and expressed in socially acceptable behaviors, anger can be adaptive. However, it gets messy when anger leads to explosions. Again, this can be discussed as an abstract concept. The actual clean up of the spilled over "hot lava" provides opportunity to discuss verbally and process tactile and visual representations of the messiness of angry explosions. The therapist also discusses the child's responsibility for how they express their anger and the consequences of it.

Procedure:

The child is introduced to the volcano model and the model is opened. The therapist introduces the concept of anger and how it is sometimes described as being like an erupting volcano. Usually, a child has heard of this analogy. The therapist then indicates that the eruption is only the most extreme of anger. It is when anger bubbles over and comes out in temper tantrums and/or verbal or physical aggression. The child's extreme anger is compared to boiling hot lava rolling down the side of the volcano. The continuum of anger from low to high is discussed. The child and therapist then make a list of at least 5 levels of intensity. The levels of anger are written on post-it notes and adhered to one-half of the inside of the separated volcano. For example, the lowest level of the volcano may be labeled "annoyed". The next "frustrated", followed by "mad/angry" and finally at the top, "rage". The child may decide on different feelings words to use on his volcano.

The other half of the volcano model is utilized to talk about coping skills that correspond to the intensity of anger. The coping skills are written on post-it notes and adhered to the side of the volcano corresponding to the level of anger it may be helpful in modulating. The child and therapist discuss that more coping skills or a higher level of coping skill may be needed to calm the higher levels of anger. For instance, it takes more coping skills to deal with being furious than to deal with being annoyed.

The therapist and child discuss how coping skills can be used to decrease or cope with anger. If the anger is not dealt with, the intensity may increase. This may be displayed in the form of a temper tantrum or aggression. This level of anger is what is referred to in the analogy as "erupting like a volcano." Often children are aware of a limited number of coping skills. Those that are understood may not be utilized or may not be done in a way that is helpful. Coping skills that are not understood by the child may be introduced and practiced in the session or future sessions. See the list of possible coping skills in Table 1.

The therapist and child prepare for the explosion by putting on old shirts to cover their clothing. The volcano is placed in a tray with newspapers or a plastic sheet under it. The therapist or child mixes the ingredients for an eruption. The baking soda (1/2 tsp) is placed into the volcano tube. The vinegar (1/4 cup), food coloring (several drops) and dish soap (1/2 Tbl) are mixed together. When the vinegar mixture is added to the volcano, the volcano will erupt. The ingredients are compared to the situations that lead to emotional eruptions of rage. For example, the baking soda may represent having to finish a book report that was put off; the vinegar, an annoying younger sibling that gets into the client's possessions; the food coloring, a friend who decides not to come for a play date because another friend asked her to go to her house; and the dish soap, being tired. The therapist and child enjoy the volcano as it erupts. The calm and playful activity played while discussing a difficult emotion may allow the child more freedom to playfully explore their anger and behaviors associated with it.

The therapist and child discuss the mess that is created and how this is similar to the messiness of dealing with an angry tantrum or the results of verbal or physical aggression. The therapist and child may play with the ingredients to see if the eruptions are more or less with different amounts of vinegar and baking soda added. The therapist and child clean up the volcano while discussing the messiness of anger.

The handout that follows can be used, or the child may want to draw a volcano. The levels of anger and the corresponding coping skills can be written down on the handout that follows to remind the child of options.

Breathing exercises: 4-square breathing.	Count to 10.
Think of something positive/fun.	Talk about it/Get your feelings out.
Think of solutions/Problem solving.	Plan for future situations that could be similar.
Talk it out using I-Statements.	Sit down.
Find a word that makes you feel calmer. Ex. Peace or Hope	Go for a walk.
Visualize your safe place.	Ask for help from someone you trust.
Think of what you are grateful for.	Read a book.
Take a deep breath. Breathe out like you are blowing bubbles.	Write a story.
Ask for a time out to calm down.	Do gentle stretches.
Do an art project to express your feelings.	Do yoga.
Think of the consequences for your anger.	Do Progressive Muscle Relaxation.
Do problem solving. Think of how you can change the situation.	Listen to music.
Take a hot bath.	Play a sport or do aerobic exercise.
Journal.	Tear up a phone book.
Play with clay.	Be assertive.
Compromise with the person.	Talk to your best friend.

Table 1: Possible coping skills which can be listed on half of the volcano.

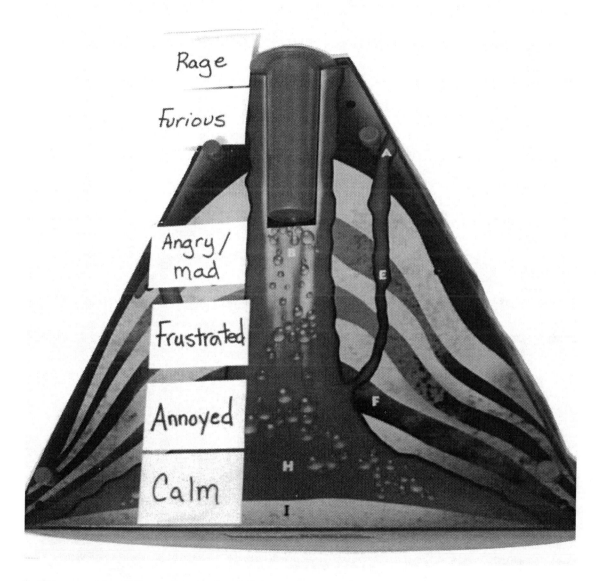

Figure 1: On one side of the volcano the child and therapist label levels of anger, across the anger continuum. The names of feelings are written on Post-it notes and placed on the volcano with the lower levels of anger at the bottom and higher levels of anger at the top.

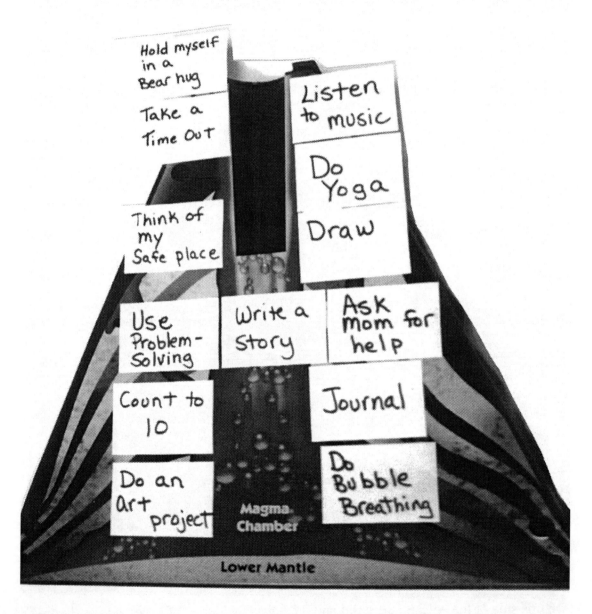

Figure 2: The other side of the volcano is labeled with coping skills written on Post-it notes and adhered to the volcano. Coping skills useful for less intense feelings of anger are adhered lower on the volcano and coping skills effective with more intense anger at the top of the volcano.

VOLCANO HANDOUT

Label anger words inside the volcano. One represents the least amount of anger. This may be annoyed. Five represents the highest level of anger. This may be rage.

List coping skills that you feel may be helpful for that level of anger. For example, "count to ten" may work at level one and "talk to someone" may work at level three.

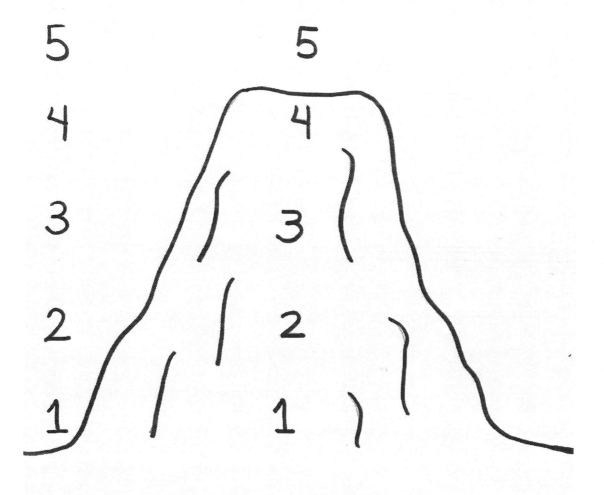

Coping Skills   Anger Words

<u>**Title**</u>: Funnel Your Anger

<u>**Treatment Theme**</u>: Feelings Identification and Modulation

<u>**Treatment Goals**</u>:
1. Provide psychoeducation about positive/constructive and negative/destructive ways anger can be expressed.
2. Provide a concrete representation of funneling while discussing the funneling of anger to positive/constructive responses to anger.
3. Provide a transitional object to represent the concept of funneling anger.

<u>**Treatment Modalities**</u>: Individual/Family/Group

<u>**Recommended Age Range**</u>: 10-18 years

<u>**Materials**</u>:
Colored Sand
Sand Art Bottles
Funnels
(All supplies are available through Discount School Supplies)

<u>**Cost of Intervention**</u>: $$

<u>**Discussion**</u>:
Children and adolescents often come to therapy due to a presenting problem that involves anger. Young clients and their caregivers may feel that anger typically is destructive in themselves and others whom they have seen angry. This intervention, and the discussion that accompanies it, is to reinforce the value of anger and how to express anger in a way that benefits the client and others.

Children and adolescents, who present in therapy with anger, often have several treatment goals related to appropriately expressing anger. There are many steps which must be addressed before exploring appropriate expression of anger. These include:
- Identification of feelings and feelings intensity
- Psychoeducation about feelings, thoughts, behaviors, and physiology
- Discussion of how anger is expressed/coping skills and
- Discussion of how anger can be funneled and used productively.

Often other play therapy interventions can be used while discussing the earlier concepts related to anger. For example, while discussing intensity of anger and using the corresponding coping skills, the Anger Volcano can be used. The Funnel Your Anger intervention is related to introducing the concept of using anger productively.

<u>**Procedure**</u>:
The therapist and client talk about ways that anger can be expressed. The concepts of lashing out, bottling, or funneling anger are discussed. This may sound like "All feelings are gifts to use that teach us about our environment and how we view it. Anger tells us that we do not feel the situation is okay.

When people are angry they tend to hold it in or lash out. However, they could funnel their anger. Funneling anger takes the energy that one has and puts it to use in a positive way. When you use a funnel with the sand, it is neater and the sand goes where you want it to. When you funnel anger, the anger can be used the way you want it to be used."

Specific examples of ways anger can be funneled are discussed with the client.

<u>Examples of how to funnel anger include:</u>
- Put your angry energy into sports.
- Express anger through music.
- Set goals so that you can change your situation.
- Use problem-solving skills.
- Learn to be more tolerant of others.
- Be assertive and stand up for yourself.
- Identify sadness and loss. Start the grieving process to let go.
- Identify jealousy. Think of how to meet needs.
- Change thoughts to be more accurate.
- Accept that some things are difficult.
- Identify a role model who used or uses anger well (i.e. for social change).
- Be a role model for others.

The client chooses sand of different colors to represent different ways that he or she has or would like to funnel anger. The color code is written down. For example:

Purple: Try to make changes in my school
Yellow: Learn to be more tolerant of others
Green: Be assertive and stand up for myself
Blue: Use my problem solving skills to change the situation
Red: Identify a role model who uses anger well/appropriately

The client then uses the colored sand and funnels it into a container such as a bottle. The amount of each color of sand represents how much they have or would like to funnel their anger in that manner. The bottle of funneled sand is given to the client as a transitional object and reminder of how they aspire to express anger in a productive manner. The handout that follows may be used.

Figure 1: A Funnel Your Anger bottle with sand in it. The sand was funneled by the child while discussing options for funneling the child's own anger.

Funnel Your Anger: Use Your Anger Productively

RESPONSES TO ANGER

1. LASHING OUT WITH ANGER is responding to anger with verbal or physical aggression.
2. BOTTLING ANGER is responding to anger by shutting down and trying to not feel.
3. FUNNELING ANGER is using anger productively.

Examples of Funneling Anger:

A. Identify a role model who uses, or has used anger well. (i.e. someone who used anger for social change).

B. Be a role model for others.

C. Identify that I am jealous that someone has something I do not, and think of how I might have my needs met.

D. Change my thoughts to be more accurate.

E. Identify sadness and loss. Start the grieving process to let go.

F. Problem-solve. Set goals so that I can change my situation.

G. Accept that some things are difficult.

H. Learn to be more tolerant of others.

I. Be assertive and stand up for myself.

J. Use your angry energy in sports.

K. Express anger through music.

Color   Ways I want to funnel anger appropriately

_____   _____

_____   _____

_____   _____

_____   _____

Title: Coping Skills Parachute

Treatment Theme: Feelings Identification and Modulation

Treatment Goals:
1. Assist the child in developing a list of possible coping skills.
2. Use a concrete representation for the metaphor of using a parachute.
3. Provide a transitional object to represent the coping skills and remind the child of the therapeutic process during which the coping skills were discussed.

Treatment Modalities: Individual/Family/Group

Recommended Age Range: 4-18 years (Adapted for developmental stage)

Materials:
Small parachute and person figure (Available through Oriental Trading Company)

Cost of Intervention: $

Discussion:
Coping skills allow a child to deal with problems and to modulate their affect. The metaphor of having a parachute is helpful for children to understand that difficulties may happen, but there are skills that can help. With adolescents, discussing having a parachute may be adequate. However, with children it is more helpful to play with the concept of falling and needing a parachute to slow the fall and protect the person.

Procedure:
The child and therapist begin by talking about parachuting. A person jumping from a plane with a parachute and gliding to the ground safely is discussed. The child is told that jumping with a parachute can even be fun! The child and therapist play with a small parachute. The therapist begins to talk about how the child may need something like a parachute to cope more adaptively. The coping skills can be those developed in therapy and those naturally used in the child's environment. The parachuted figure is tossed from different heights in the office, or if possible, from other places that allow for greater heights from which to parachute. (The safety of the child and others needs to be considered when deciding whether to use spaces such as stair cases or balconies.) Each time the parachute reaches the ground, a coping skill is written by the child on the parachute. Although this same concept can be written on a handout, this intervention allows the child to experience the concept and have fun. The child may use the parachute as both a metaphorical and practical reminder of his or her coping skills.

Relaxation

or

Mindfulness

Title: Mindful Tasting: The Taste of Emotions

Treatment Theme: Relaxation or Mindfulness

Treatment Goals:
1. Describe the concept of Mindfulness.
2. Describe the difference between Mindfulness and imagery.
3. Guide the child in experiencing being Mindful in the session.
4. Discuss the ability to tolerate feelings.

Treatment Modalities: Individual/Family/Group

Recommended Age Range: 8-18 years

Materials:
Tabasco sauce
Chocolate candies
Lemon juice or sour candies

Cost of Intervention: $

Discussion:

Twenty-five hundred years ago, a process of meditation called Mindfulness, that focused on experiencing "what is" was developed within Buddhism (Gunaratana, 2002). Mindfulness is being fully aware of the present. When one is Mindful, one focuses on the experience, not on judgment of the experience or of that which is experienced. As there is not judgment, there is no conceptualizaton of "good" or "bad" experience or event. It is accepting the moment as it is.

Psychology has utilized the powers of Mindfulness which has been incorporated into several different Cognitive Behavioral Therapies including, Dialectical Behavior Therapy (DBT), Mindfulness-Based Cognitive Therapy (M-BCT), Mindfulness-Based Stress Reduction (M-BSR), and Acceptance and Commitment Therapy (ACT) (Twohig, M.P., Field, C.E., Armstrong, A.B., & Dahl, A.L., 2010). Mindfulness has been utilized with children with internalizing and externalizing problems. The goals of learning Mindfulness in DBT include learning to tolerate feelings of distress, becoming aware of the present experiences, and learning to direct attention (Woodbury, K.A., Roy, R., Indik, J., 2008). Within M-BSR, Mindfulness is utilized with the goals of reducing anxiety and depression, and increasing positive affect and increasing self-regulation (Saltzman & Goldin, 2008).

It may be important when using Mindfulness with children and adolescents, to provide information to the client and their parents about how Mindfulness is different from imagery. Unlike imagery, where one may focus on a positive memory, mindfulness is not trying to escape the anxiety by thinking of something positive or relaxing. Mindfulness allows an older child or adolescent to understand that negative feelings can be tolerated. Negative memories and the associated feelings must be tolerated in order to heal from them.

Several specific Mindfulness interventions have been developed within CBT theories to address specific issues and make abstract concepts more understandable. A Mindfulness intervention utilizing Chinese handcuffs is helpful in teaching children that one does not need to follow through with what they may first want to do, which is likely to be pulling away (Hays, et.al., 1999). The child plays with the Chinese handcuffs and processes how one does not have to go with the first behavior that might be considered. When the child puts his or her fingers in the handcuffs the first impulse may be to pull their fingers out. However to be released, the child must push his or her fingers in. This intervention teaches the child to stop his or her impulsive behavior and become aware of the situation.

Mindful Eating is a concept that has been utilized to provide insight into awareness with the focus on the present moment (Semple, R.J. & Lee, J., 2008). When Mindfully Eating, one focuses on the experience before and after taking a bite. It is a multisensory experience with a bite taking a significant amount of time (Saltzman & Goldin, 2008). An example is the Mindfully Eating a Raisin Exercise (Semple, 2005 as referenced in Semple & Lee, 2008). The Mindful Eating: The Taste of Emotions intervention builds on the concept of Mindful Eating to include teaching the concept of being Mindful despite the emotions which are being experienced.

Utilizing Mindfulness with younger clients has many similarities to how it is taught to adults. Mindfulness is done through experiential activities in therapy and some didactic training (Twohig, M.P., Field, C.E., Armstrong, A.B., & Dahl, A.L., 2010) with adults. This is similar to how Mindfulness is taught to children. With both children and adults, Mindfulness is practiced in and outside of sessions. Essential to practicing Mindfulness with children is the incorporation of their parents in the process. Parents can learn and use the skills, encourage practice and assist in the generalization of skills. Mindfulness has been utilized mostly with adults and the research conducted on effectiveness thereof has been done mostly on adults. However, there are some studies indicating that Mindfulness is helpful in treating children and adolescents. Most studies have been done on adolescents than children. These studies have focused on Mindfulness within a program (i.e., DBT). Therefore the factors that make Mindfulness effective may not generalize to Mindfulness interventions utilized independently of a program. However, it is likely that Mindfulness interventions can be beneficial.

Clinicians who utilize Mindfulness typically practice mindfulness themselves and may take part in the Mindful activities. This allows for joint processing with the child.

Procedure:
First the concept of Mindfulness is described to the child or adolescent. For example, the older child or adolescent is told a definition of Mindfulness such as, "Mindfulness is accepting the present situation without trying to change it. It is full awareness of and experiencing of the situation at that moment. When being Mindfulness one does not judge it." For children, Mindfulness is explained as just doing something and focusing on it. The child is told that when being Mindful he or she just does it and does not think about whether it is a "good or bad" experience or event.

The client is offered a small chocolate candy. The client is asked to focus on holding the piece of candy. The client is asked to think about how hard or soft it is. The client is asked to focus on how it smells. Whether the client's mouth has started to water is processed as a part of the experience of eating a chocolate. The client then puts the candy in his or her mouth. The client is asked to suck on the chocolate candy for two minutes while just focusing on the experience. If the client feels comfortable with closed eyes, they are asked to close them. The client is asked to think about the texture of the candy and the flavor. The client is asked to attend to the whether his or her cheeks are sucked in and what happens to the candy such as whether it "melts" in his or her mouth. The client and therapist focus on the taste for a couple of minutes.

After the client has experienced the Mindful Eating of chocolate, the therapist and child discuss foods or flavors that can be associated with different feelings. The chocolate candy may represent love and happiness. Lemon juice may represent jealousy and sorrow. Tabasco sauce may represent frustration (mild sauce) anger (medium) and rage (hot). The client is asked to think of other food/feeling associations. It is usually helpful to have the bottles present as visual cues representing the tastes. **However, the lemon juice and the Tabasco sauce are not tasted by the client unless they request to do so.**

The concept of tolerating feelings is explored further. A client may have an uncomfortable feeling such as sorrow, but does not have to do something about it. This is compared to the ability to tolerate tastes that are not pleasurable. The child may be told:

The taste of lemon juice can be tolerated; one does not have to spit it out. Sorrow is not enjoyable but does not need to be avoided. Sorrow, like lemon juice, can be tolerated. At times, avoiding sorrow is done at a high cost. For example, one may avoid a feeling by using coping skills that are detrimental to the client, such as holding in sadness and becoming depressed, or acting out with aggression.

The client is encouraged to accept his or her feelings instead of pushing them away. The therapist checks-in over future sessions on the client's ability to experience feelings in a Mindful manner. The last few minutes of future sessions can include being Mindful of the positive feelings while Mindfully Eating a chocolate together.

Gunarantana, B.H. (2002). *Mindfulness in plain English.* Somerville, MA: Wisdom Publications.

Hayes, S.C., Strosahl, K.D., & Wilson, K.G. (1999). *Acceptance and commitment therapy: An experiential therapy to behavior change.* New York: Guilford.

Saltzman, A. & Goldin, P. (2008). Mindfulness-based stress reduction for school-aged children. In: L.A. Greco, & S.C. Hayes (Eds.), *Acceptance and mindfulness treatment for children and adolescents: A practitioner's guide.* Oakland, CA: New Harbinger.

Semple, R.J. & Lee, J. (2008). Treating anxiety with mindfulness: Mindfulness-Based Cognitive Therapy for children. In: L.A. Greco & S.C. Hayes (Eds.), *Acceptance and mindfulness treatment for children and adolescents: A practitioner's guide.* Oakland, CA: New Harbinger.

Twohig, M.P., Field, C.E., Armstrong, A.B., & Dahl, A.L. (2010). Acceptance and mindfulness as mechanisms of change in Mindfulness-Based interventions for children and adolescents. In: R.A. Baer (Ed.), *Assessing mindfulness and acceptance processes in clients: Illuminating the theory and practice of change.* Oakland: New Harbinger Press.

Woodbury, K.A., Roy, R., & Indik, J. (2008). Dialectical behavior therapy for adolescents with borderline features. In: L.A. Greco, & S.C. Hayes (Eds.), *Acceptance and mindfulness treatment for children and adolescents: A practitioner's guide.* Oakland, CA: New Harbinger.

Title: Two Playful Interventions for Learning Progressive Muscle Relaxation (PMR):
Progressive Muscle Relaxation *From Head to Toe*: Game Playing to Shape PMR and
The Tighten and Relax Dance

Treatment Theme: Relaxation or Mindfulness

Treatment Goals:
1. Teach the concept of PMR.
2. Engage the child in a playful game that can be modified through shaping to closer and closer approximations to PMR.
3. Increase the child's use of PMR as a positive coping skill.

Treatment Modalities: Individual/Family/Group

Recommended Age Range: 2-8 years of age

Materials:
A hard toy such as a large action figure
A soft, toy preferably a flat stuffed animal with floppy limbs
From Head to Toe: Learn to Move Game (Available at department stores in the toy section)
  From Head to Toe by Eric Carle, copyright ©1997 by Eric Carle.
  Used with permission from the Eric Carle Studio.

Cost of Intervention: $$

Discussion:
Progressive Muscle Relaxation can reduce anxiety and anger and help children learn to relax to fall asleep. The child may approximate PMR by contracting and relaxing muscle groups (O'Connor, 1991). O'Connor suggests that children may benefit from PMR if able to follow directions and focus. The following exercise is a playful way to engage children in the PMR process, to increase focus, compliance, and enjoyment.

It is important to teach relaxation in an engaging and enjoyable manner. It is very difficult to relax when one does not want to do so, since resistance is counter to relaxation. When children are taught relaxation, they willingly participate in the activity. Therefore, PMR may need to be done in progressive approximations, especially for resistant children. PMR works best with practice and the child may engage in PMR homework if they enjoy it.

The parent is an important partner in teaching PMR. It works best when the child and parent playfully engage together in PMR as a desired activity. Often it is helpful to request that the parent have the child do PMR when it is most likely that the child will want to do it and when the child is calm.

When children have been traumatized, treatment typically includes psychoeducation related to anxiety reduction techniques such as PMR. When the child has learned to reduce anxiety including the physiological responses (i.e., increased heart rate, muscle tension), he or she can begin using the skill when engaging in trauma-specific interventions. Likewise, when the child has problems with anger, PMR needs to be learned when the child is calm and relaxed first. Later, the parent can have the child use PMR when mildly annoyed but not angry. Often parents will say that PMR did not work but will say they only told the child to use it when the child was already in the thralls of a raging temper tantrum or highly anxious. Likewise, for children who use PMR to help relax before bedtime, it is helpful to have the child practice at other times as well.

The following two interventions apply similar concepts. In both, progressive approximations of behavior are done to teach the child to do PMR. In the first, the game *From Head to Toe* is utilized. The cards show movements that can be done with children learning PMR. See Figure 1. In the second, hard and soft toys are utilized and the therapist and child do a Tighten and Relax Dance. Often the therapist may want to use a combination of both depending upon the individual child's needs.

Toys are beneficial in teaching the concepts of tense and relaxed. The game *From Head to Toe*, allows the child to enjoy playing a fun game. The game consists of cards of beautiful, colorful pictures of children doing movements. The cards are drawn by players and the movements done. The movements include many that are similar to flexing a muscle group which makes it helpful in teaching PMR.

Toys that can represent relaxed (soft and floppy) and toys which represent tense (hard) help the child understand the concepts of PMR. The following interventions use toys and play to teach Progressive Muscle Relaxation.

From Head to Toe: Learn to Move Eric Carle Game

O'Connor, K. (1997). Using Guided Imagery to Augment the Play Therapy Process In: Kaduson, H & Schaefer, C. (Eds.), *101 Favorite Play Therapy Techniques.* pp. 6-10. Northvale, NJ: Jason Aronson Inc.

O'Connor, K. (1991). *The Play Therapy Primer.* New York: Wiley.

Progressive Muscle Relaxation From Head to Toe: Game Playing to Shape PMR

The game *From Head to Toe* is introduced to the child. For the most resistant children, the cards are drawn and the actions played out by the child and therapist. Often this works best when both therapist and child perform each card. The activity may be the focus of the session for only five or ten minutes depending upon attention span. However, if the therapist demonstrates the moves to an attentive, though non-participating child, the length can be longer. After doing the moves standing, the therapist lies on the floor or sits in a chair. The moves are adapted to this position. Each step is done with statements about how the muscles are moving and working. Following each step, the therapist talks about and demonstrates the muscles being floppy. A floppy toy may be used to demonstrate the relaxed state. The therapist and child go through each muscle group (or four or five are chosen by the therapist to focus on muscle groups from head to toe) tightening and relaxing each group. The From Head to Toe cards are held at the therapist's side and shown to the child if needed. As the therapist and child do the relaxation over time, the child will likely be able to remember and do several muscle groups without the cards. Parents are included in the activity as clinically indicated. When parents are able to help the child relax, they may be included from the introduction of PMR. At times it is more helpful to videotape the intervention being done with the child, perhaps over several sessions. This videotape can be beneficial in teaching parents to be calm, relaxed, and playful in teaching the concept. Parents may be encouraged to purchase the cards for use in the home.

Figure 1: Eric Carle's game *From Head to Toe*. The game is played with the child with movements alternating with relaxation. Shaping is used to learn Progressive Muscle Relaxation.
Used with the permission of Eric Carle.

The Tighten and Relax Dance:

The Tighten and Relax Dance is another fun activity to teach PMR. First the therapist introduces a toy, such as a large action figure, that is made of hard material, such as hard plastic. The therapist comments on the hard features of the toy. These comments are focused on muscle groups from the toy's head to its feet. For example, the therapist will say, "Look at Strong Man's face. See how hard it is! Oh, my! I am going to touch his face. It is very hard. Do you want to touch it?" The child is encouraged to touch and discuss the hardness. The child is then shown a floppy toy such as a flat, soft, floppy stuffed animal. The therapist encourages the child to touch and talk about the soft toy as well.

The therapist then tells the child that she or he is going to do a Tight Dance. The therapist dances stiffly in a circle with tight muscles. The child is invited to participate in the dance. If indicated, the parent is invited to participate. The therapist then performs a Tight March and marches with stiff, tight muscles. The therapist then indicates a Floppy Dance/March is next and proceeds to dance in a loose manner and finishes with a flop into a beanbag or chair. The child and therapist do the Tighten and Relax Dance/March several times at the rate which seems to engage the child. The therapist then lies on the floor and tightens and relaxes his or her muscles. The child is encouraged to participate at this point as well. At first, the PMR on the floor may need to consist of only a few or several muscle groups and the steps should proceed swiftly to keep the child's attention. The number of muscle groups can increase and the speed of the process can be increased. Some children are able to play the game and begin to grasp PMR in one or two sessions. Other children may require multiple sessions.

After introducing the concept, personalization of the relaxation lesson may include asking the parent and child to bring the child's own "tense" and "relaxed" toys. Ask the parents to help the child find a soft, plush toy that represents relaxed and a hard, tense, tight toy that represents tense such as an action figure at home. Have the child and parent bring the toys to the next session. Ask parents to do the Tighten and Relax Dance at home emphasizing the playful manner in which to do it.

Interventions Related to Emotions, Thoughts, and Behaviors

Title: Magnetic Cognitive Triangle

Treatment Theme: Interventions Related to Emotions, Thoughts, and Behaviors

Treatment Goals:
1. Provide psychoeducation related to the Cognitive Triangle including the connection between feelings, thoughts and behaviors.
2. Provide objects (magnets) to the child which represent feelings, thoughts, behaviors, and triggers/ antecedents that the child can physically manipulate.
3. Provide a self-correcting therapeutic tool which differentiates feelings, thoughts, behaviors, and triggers/antecedents from each other.
4. Normalize responses to life events (trauma, divorce, peer problems) by providing examples of common feelings, thoughts, and behaviors associated with these events.
5. Provide psychoeducation about changing thoughts and assist the child in replacing negative thoughts.
6. Provide psychoeducation related to how changing thoughts can change feelings and behaviors.

Treatment Modalities: Individual

Recommended Age Range: 6 years-Adult

Materials:
Large Magnetic board
Magnets (Use any four shapes and sizes to differentiate between the categories. For consistency, the following colors and shapes were associated with the following categories throughout this description of the intervention.)
- Feelings: Blue Triangles
- Behaviors: Red Trapezoids
- Thoughts: Yellow Octagons
- Triggers/Antecedents: Orange Diamonds
Fine tip permanent marker
Cognitive Triangle handout
Lists of Feelings, Thoughts, Behaviors, and Triggers

Cost of Intervention: $$$

Advanced Preparation:
On the magnetic board, draw a large triangle in the center with ample space on every side. Label each of the corners of the triangle with the words "Feeling", "Thinking," and "Doing/Actions," or use a symbol for each. Feeling may be represented with a heart, thinking with a brain, and doing with a body shape that appears to be moving by drawing little lines by the arms and legs. In a corner, draw a square and label it "Triggers" or "Antecedents". See Figure 1 for an example of the magnetic triangle. Figures 2-5 are templates for the triangle, heart (Feeling), brain (Thinking) and body moving (Doing/Actions). Magnets of four colors and shapes are utilized to represent feeling, thinking, behavior, and triggers/antecedents. For example, yellow octagons may represent thinking. However any color or shape of magnet may be chosen by the therapist. It works best to have a larger magnet represent thoughts since the thoughts tend to require more words than triggers, feelings, or behaviors.

Magnets are prepared by writing common feelings, thoughts, and behaviors on the magnets. Figures 10-18 include thoughts, behaviors, feelings, and triggers that may be used on magnets. The lists that follow have often been noted by children and adolescents in therapy. Blank magnets for additions are highly recommended. See Figure 6 for examples of magnets representing each of the categories.

Discussion:

Cognitive Behavioral Play Therapy (CBPT) is based on the premise that the child's cognitions impact his or her feelings and behaviors (Knell, 1993). Cognitive Behavioral Therapy (CBT) is limited by the child's cognitive development. However, through play, the concepts and strategies used in CBT can be adapted for use with children (Knell, 1993). The cognitive triangle represents an abstract concept, the relationships between one's feelings, thoughts and behaviors. Through play with the Magnetic Cognitive Triangle, the abstract concept can be processed. On the Magnetic Cognitive Triangle, categories are represented with a symbol to assist the client in remembering the categories. The tactile experience of touching and moving the magnets seems helpful as well.

Both common and individualized responses are present as magnetic options for selection. The Magnetic Cognitive Triangle allows for normalization of feelings, thoughts, and behaviors. When the child sees numerous positive and negative thoughts and behaviors, he or she realizes these have been experienced by other children. Clinical discretion may be utilized in deciding which premade magnets the clinician wants to include. The options allow children to pick descriptions of their experiences that are consistent with their perceptions.

The fourth category of magnets is Triggers or Antecedents. This category may be necessary for some but not all cases. Triggers are often highly individual, based on the client's experience of trauma. Keep magnets of a child's specific triggers separate from other magnets. It is helpful to process each category (feelings, thoughts, behaviors and triggers) individually before applying it to a situation.

The Magnetic Cognitive Triangle can be helpful in reaching several therapeutic goals.
It may be used during psychoeducation related to feelings. A child may not have good recall of an extensive list of feelings when processing an incident. Twenty to thirty feelings listed on magnets allow for accuracy in expressing the child's experience. In an early session with the Magnetic Cognitive Triangle, the therapist can use the board and magnets to review feelings, typical physiology associated with the feeling, and common scenarios when someone may feel that feeling. The feelings that are related can be put into feelings families. The child can put the feelings in order from least to most intense. For example, for the angry family the child may order the continuum from annoyed to frustrated to angry to rage.

The Magnetic Cognitive Triangle can be helpful in teaching about how thoughts influence feelings and how feelings influence behavior. The child can also process how he or she can change his or her thoughts to alternative thoughts. The connections, drawn on the board, are a visual of the relationships between feelings, thoughts and behaviors. In addition, as the child discusses situations, it is helpful to discuss the relationship between them. The child's thoughts and alternative thoughts can be processed using the Magnetic Cognitive Triangle. This is based on the CBT premise that one can determine his or her thoughts and that the thoughts impact feelings and behaviors (Knell, 1993). When a child adds a thought to a magnet it may be helpful to add alternative thoughts to magnets so that more adaptive, positive options are available to process. Often children will add alternative thoughts themselves as they become more experienced in processing with the Magnetic Cognitive Triangle. In thinking about automatic thoughts and alternative thoughts, the therapist discusses how each thought impacts feelings and behaviors.

The Magnetic Cognitive Triangle is helpful as it allows the child to self-correct. When teaching the cognitive triangle, children often make numerous mistakes about feelings, thoughts and behaviors. For example, children often mislabel feelings as thoughts or vice versa such as, "I was thinking I'm really mad," or, "I was feeling like I should not have to share my birthday presents with my brother." The self correcting nature of the Magnetic Triangle frees the child to process feelings, thoughts and behaviors. When a playful tool is not available during this discussion, children often allow themselves only a few mistakes before limiting their learning due to not wanting to make mistakes. With the Magnetic Cognitive Triangle, the child can see options from each category.

The Magnetic Cognitive Triangle allows the child to process common feelings, thoughts, and behaviors as well as contributing their own subjective experiences to the activity. Initially the Magnetic Cognitive Triangle is helpful as a starting point with the existing magnets. Additional magnets which reflect individual client's specific thoughts, feelings, behaviors, and triggers can be continually added. When adding to the responses, clinical discretion is recommended. Specifically, some behaviors or thoughts may be more therapeutic when divided into specific categories. For example, common thoughts and behaviors of children with attachment disorders or sexually abused children may be more useful with some clients than with others. However, these magnets may be removed for other clients depending, for example, upon age and presenting problem. Magnets that are specific to a particular client may be kept separately from the others.

The Magnetic Cognitive Triangle is helpful in assisting children in processing information that they want to resist processing. Often more emotionally difficult material is more difficult to talk about. The Magnetic Cognitive Triangle allows the child to process the information in steps. Initially the child may process it through picking magnets. Without the Magnetic Cognitive Triangle, children may be more like to say that they do not know or they may give short, incomplete responses when discussing situations. With the Magnetic Cognitive Triangle, clients are more likely to begin the processing with the assistance of options as well as the nonverbal method of expression. As the situation is processed further, it is helpful to have the child talk through the magnets chosen and how the categories (Feelings, Thoughts, Behaviors, Triggers/Antecedents) relate to each other.

Knell, S. M. (1993). *Cognitive Behavioral Play Therapy*. Northvale, NJ: Jason Aronson, Inc.

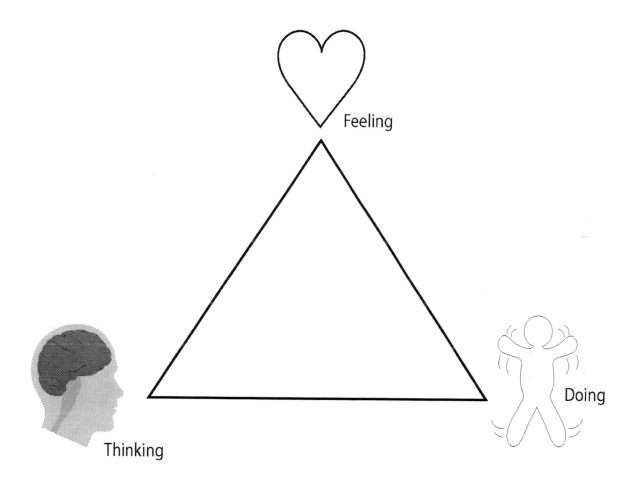

Figure 1: The magnetic board with a triangle, heart, brain and 'moving' person drawn on it. Feelings, Thinking, and Doing may also be labeled.

On the pages that follow, Figures 2-5 are templates for the triangle, brain (Thinking), person moving (Doing/Actions) and heart (Feeling).

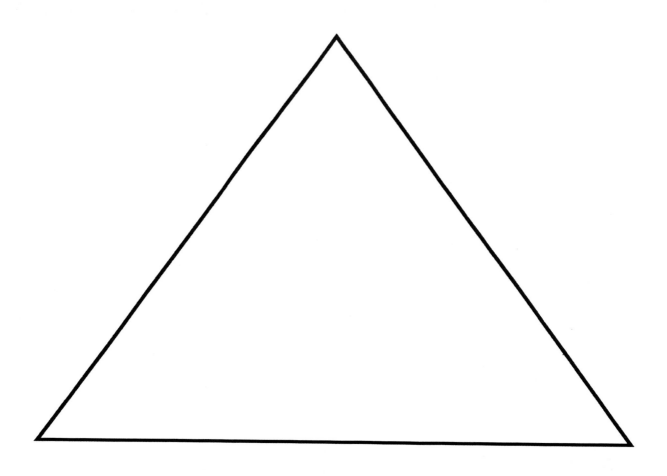

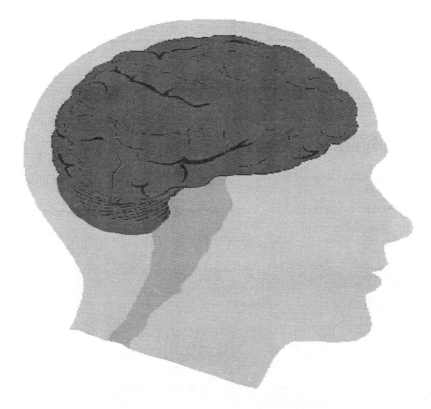

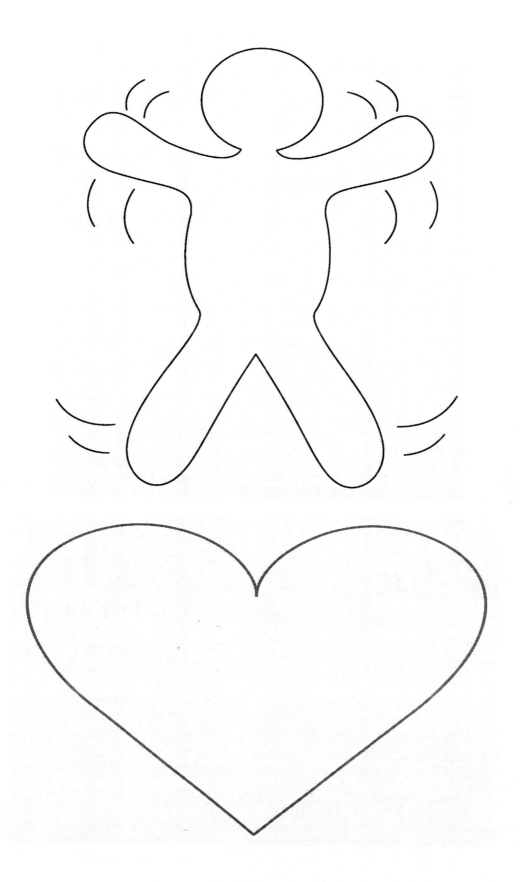

Figure 6: Magnets representing feelings, triggers, behaviors, and thoughts.

Procedure:

This intervention may be utilized for several different therapeutic goals. It is a tool which can be utilized differently in different sessions. Initially, the child is introduced to the Cognitive Triangle using the Magnetic Cognitive Triangle. The relationships between feelings, thoughts, and behaviors are discussed. Typically, the additional category of triggers/antecedents may be discussed in a later session. When first introduced, it may be helpful to use the Magnetic Triangle to process feelings. The various feelings may be discussed, including what feelings mean, how they are experienced in the body, and common situations when one may experience a feeling are discussed. Feelings expression is processed with the therapist and child, showing how people look when experiencing different feelings. Feelings can be grouped according to feelings families and continuums of feelings using the magnets.

After the child has an understanding of the three (or four if triggers are used) categories and the relationships between them, a specific situation can be processed using the Magnetic Cognitive Triangle. The child takes the feelings magnets that represent feelings he or she felt in the situation. Feelings magnets are placed in the triangle. Next, the child is asked to find magnets or make new magnets that represent his or her behavior in the situation. Finally, thoughts magnets are chosen. The child places the magnets in the triangle. The child processes each category as they choose the magnets. Triggers and antecedents magnets are chosen and placed inside the triangle. The child may choose additional magnets for any category as they process the situation. Often with further discussion, clients return to a category and add additional magnets.

After the magnets depicting the categories are chosen, the child processes the situation. Nonverbal behaviors are observed throughout the session. For example, some children seem to need to move the magnets as they talk and some organize them into designs.

To process a specific incident, the child is asked to tell about it. The magnets he or she placed on the board are utilized to tell an accurate and full narrative of the event he or she is processing. Alternative feelings, thoughts, and behaviors are processed. How the alternative thoughts led to a different affective outcome are processed. The child may take the magnets that represent the behaviors in which he or she wishes he or she had engaged.

As children utilize the Magnetic Cognitive Triangle, they learn to order their magnets on the board and this seems to correlate with a more organized verbal description of the event as well. Often the feelings, thoughts, and behaviors weave throughout their narrative of the situations they process using the board. They may be able to make more connections and start to articulate how they could have different thoughts and change their own feelings. They also become better able to process how they may have a trigger, or a feeling, or a thought, but they still get to decide what behavior they will choose. The order of magnetic choices typically works well from feelings to behaviors to thoughts. However, the clinician can decide upon a different order.

An example of a child processing a situation with the Magnetic Cognitive Triangle follows.
The child said she was mad because she wanted to have a sleepover. She picked the following feelings: mad, angry, annoyed, and sad. She picked the following thoughts: "This is not fair", "I must be able to have a sleep-over", and "I never get what I want". She picked the behaviors that she had: yelling, demanding, having a temper tantrum and isolating. In the session, her thoughts were processed. It was discussed that her thoughts have words in them such as "never" that often relate to feeling mad or sad. Alternative thoughts are processed including: "Sometimes I do not get what I want" and "I would like to have a sleep-over but I don't need to have one". She was then able to indicate that her changed

thoughts related to having a less intense feeling of frustration. She indicated that had she changed her thoughts and feelings at the time of the incident, she would have shown behaviors such as pouting or taking a break instead of having a temper tantrum. Her behaviors were also processed including how her behavior related to her thinking and feeling. How her behavior impacted the likelihood of future sleep-overs was also discussed.

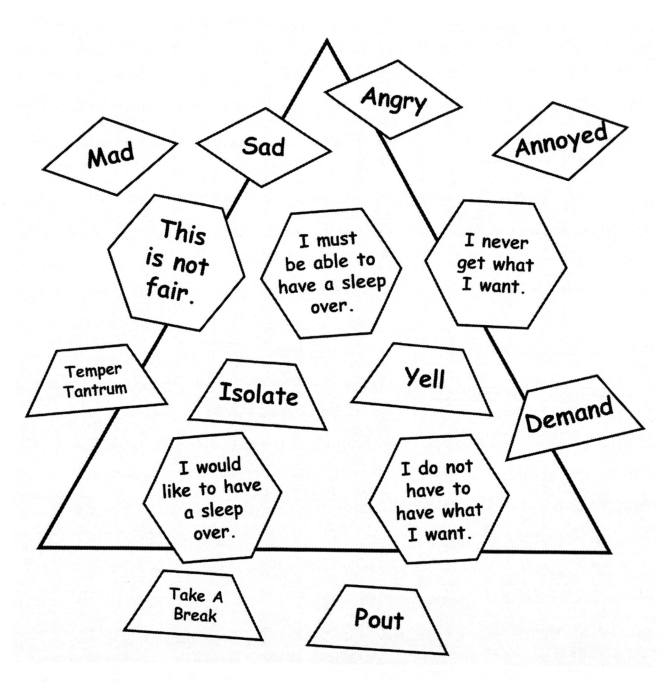

Figure 7: A drawing of the Magnetic Cognitive Triangle with an example of a child's magnets attached.

Another example follows. See Figures 8 and 9. This example includes triggers and the reactions of the child:

> *"The smell of alcohol was the trigger. I smelled it and I started to feel scared and sad. I felt kind of alone, too. Then I started thinking about how my mom has not been there for me and how I am not loved. I cried and I went into my room. Then I thought that my grandma loves me and it is not my fault that my mom has not been able to take care of me. Then I may still feel alone but I feel less sad. I go out of my room and talk with grandma. Then I feel ok.*

This situation may result in similar but less intense feelings after the child changed the focus of her thoughts. The therapist talks to the child about his or her ability to make decisions about what thoughts to focus on. The child is reminded that by changing thoughts and feelings, they have more control over behaviors. The therapist can also discuss the consequences of behaviors and how the child may want to make changes in thinking and feeling earlier. The child and therapist can discuss the trigger and how it may influence feelings and thoughts. Also, the child is encouraged to make changes as soon as triggers are noticed. The child is encouraged to think of triggers as something to notice and respond to, by actively changing thinking and feeling and ultimately changing behaviors. While processing scenarios with the Magnetic Cognitive Triangle, the child is encouraged to take control of their thinking, feelings and behaving.

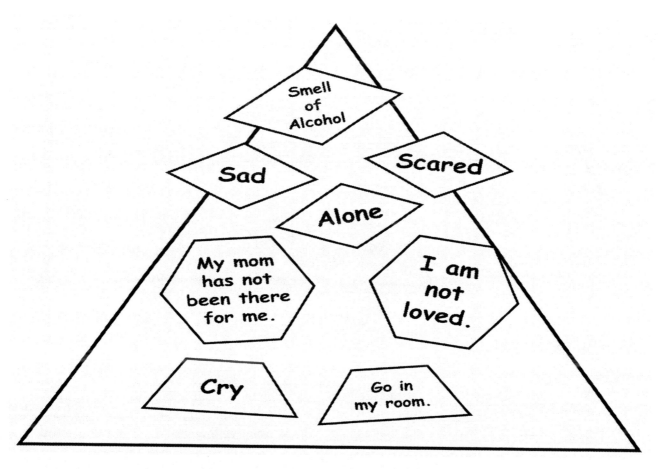

Figure 8: The child's initial processing using the Magnetic Cognitive Triangle. The child has given her trigger, feelings, thoughts and behaviors.

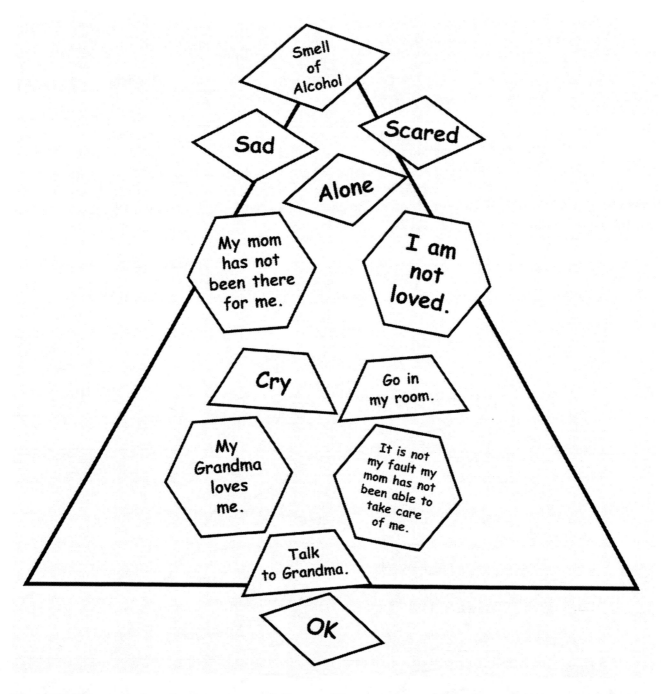

Figure 9: The example was restructured using the cognitive triangle. The child was able to consider alternative thoughts after thinking about the situation. The feelings that accompanied the changes in thoughts are noted with the blue diamonds that followed the alternative thoughts.

Figure 10: Behaviors Therapists may choose to write the following behaviors on Red Trapezoids. Additional behaviors can be added by clients or therapists as needed.

Ask for help	Act disrespectfully	Ask for what I need	Breathe	Budge in line	Bubble Breathing
Be assertive	Bump into someone	Bite	Calm myself	Count to 10	Cover up with blanket
Cry	Complain	Do school work	Distract myself	Do relaxation	Deep breathing
Don't do school work	Deep breathing	Demand	Do a puzzle	Do yoga	Exercise
Fantasize	Focus on the trigger	Focus on others	Go to Mom	Get jumpy	Go fishing
Get sassy	Go for a walk	Get backrub	Go to school	Go to Dad	Go for a walk
Hurt myself	Hide	Hit	Hug	Have hot chocolate	Hug Dad
Hug mom	Hug a friend	Isolate	Ignore	Jump	Listen to calming music
Listen to teacher	Listen to audio book	Listen to classical music	Let it go	Tell a Lie	Listen to a relaxation CD
Listen to adults	Listen to mom	Listen to dad	Listen to loud music	Listen to mom	Let myself feel it
Leave the situation	Make an I-statement	Make a goal	Meditate	Make cookies	Kick
Progressive Muscle Relaxation	Play with hamster	Pet my cat	Pet my dog	Plan	Pray
Play	Pout	Play cards	Play basketball	Play football	Punch
Pull away	Run away	Read	Reject my mom	Run	Read Bible
Read Koran	Refuse to talk	Refuse to do what adults tell me	Stretch	Say mean things to myself	Say "thank you"
Say "I am sorry"	Say mean things to others	Say nothing	Stay quiet	Study	Stay home

Scream	Say "I love you"	Shuffle cards	Slap	Swim	Swear
Tease	Talk	Tell the other person to stop	Throw a chair	Tell her to stop	Turn on lights
Talk to a friend	Talk to a parent	Tell a teacher	Tell dad	Tell someone	Think positively
Think of my safe place.	Tell Mom	Throw things	Use distraction	Use problem solving	Visualize the future
Walk the dog	Walk away	Watch a movie	Watch fish	Write a song	Yell

Figure 11: Feelings Therapists may choose to write the following feelings on Blue Diamonds. Add other feelings as needed.

Annoyed	Anxious	Ashamed	Angry	Agonized	Arrogant
Aggressive	Apologetic	Bored	Bashful	Concentrating	Crazy
Cool	Content	Confident	Cautious	Careless	Confused
Cold	Calm	Curious	Crabby	Disbelieving	Disappointed
Depressed	Disgusted	Distasteful	Determined	Envious	Exhausted
Exasperated	Excited	Ecstatic	Embarrassed	Fearful	Freaked out
Frightened	Empty	Hurt	Guilty	Grieving	Happy
Hot	Frustrated	Horrified	Hopeful	Hysterical	Impatient
Irritable	Homesick	Indifferent	Joyful	Jealous	Lonesome
Lovestruck	Interested	Lonely	Miserable	Meditative	Mischievous
Negative	Mad	Nervous	Obstinate	Proud	In Pain
Optimistic	Overwhelmed	OK	Puzzled	Paranoid	Pained
Perplexed	Enraged	Puzzled	Relaxed	Regret	Surly
Sympathetic	Suspicious	Smug	Shocked	Relieved	Stubborn
Sad	Surprised	Scared	Shy	Sensitive	Thoughtful
Satisfied	Tired	Sheepish	Upset	Worried	Withdrawn

Figure 12: Triggers Therapists may choose to write these triggers on Orange Triangles. Additional triangles can be added as needed.

Being told "no"	Birthday	Being punished	Christmas	Hymns from funeral	Loud noises
Hugs	Quick movements	Smell of cologne	Smell of cigarettes	Smell of candy	Smell of alcohol
Sassy peers	Toys given by perpetrator	Thunder	Time out	Unlocked windows and doors	Yelling
Men	Certain songs	Mom going to work	Holiday music	Slimy foods	Smell of body odor

Figure 13: Thoughts Therapists may choose to write the following thoughts on Yellow Octagons. Additional thoughts can be added as needed. Thoughts common for victims of abuse when considering disclosure:

If I tell, the person abusing me will go to jail.	If I tell, I may feel embarrassed. I don't want to feel embarrassed.
If I tell, it may hurt me.	If I tell, my mom may choose to stay with him, not me.
If I tell, it may hurt my mom/sister/other family member.	I don't want people to know the gross stuff I had to do. If I tell, they may know.
If I tell, the person touching me may be hurt.	I have told before and no one believed me.
I love the person that is touching me.	If I tell, my mom (or other family member) will think I am a trouble maker.
I don't know if people will believe me.	I have lied about other things and people will not believe this.
My family will change if I tell.	At first, it seemed innocent. I liked it then, so it must be my fault.
If I tell, we won't have enough money. The person touching me works to support our family.	I may not need to tell. Perhaps if I don't tell, it may just stop.
We may not be able to keep living in our home if I tell.	If I tell, I may get in trouble. Maybe it is my fault too.
My mom (or other family member) will not believe me anyway.	If I tell, I will not get privileges that I get now.
Some of it felt good. It must be my fault.	I accepted gifts so it must be my fault.

Figure 14: Thoughts Therapists may choose to write the following thoughts on Yellow Octagons. Additional thoughts can be added as needed. Thoughts related to disclosure of abuse:

If I tell, I will not have to continue being abused.	If I tell, I will help him get help for his problems.
If I tell, the person abusing me will not be able to abuse others.	If I tell, I will be able to help my family heal.
If I tell, I will be protected.	If I tell, I am brave.

Figure 15: Thoughts Therapists may choose to write the following thoughts on Yellow Octagons. Additional thoughts can be added as needed. Thoughts related to child abuse and self blame.

I didn't tell right away so it must be my fault.	I liked the attention so it must be my fault.
I didn't tell him to stop so it must be my fault.	I could have stopped it.
I don't want anyone to touch me.	I liked the privileges I got, so it must be my fault.
I hurt my whole family because I was abused.	It is my dad's fault.
The abuse is not happening now.	I am damaged because of the abuse.
I am there (where the abuse happened).	I am in a safe place.

Figure 16: Thoughts Therapists may choose to write the following thoughts on Yellow Octagons. Additional thoughts can be added as needed. Thoughts related to behavioral problems, depression, and anxiety:

I have way too much to do.	I can take it one step at a time.
I can get through this.	Sometimes I do not get what I want.
I need to be perfect.	I am good enough.
I am bad.	I am good.
I should not have done that.	I could have made a better choice.
This is not fair.	This is fair.
I was not responsible for it.	I was responsible for it.
I don't want to listen to anyone.	Many conflicts contribute to how my life is now.
Everything is my fault.	I am responsible for my behavior.
It was dumb that they did that.	Sometimes they do things wrong.
It was dumb that I did that.	Sometimes I do things wrong.
Sometimes others make mistakes.	Sometimes I make mistakes.
I need to be perfect.	I don't have to be perfect.
I'm not good enough.	Nobody is perfect.
I don't want others to demand things of me.	I can be a member of the group.
I want him or her to give me something.	It is okay for others not to share.
I don't do anything right.	Nobody likes me.
I must be able to have a sleep-over.	I value myself.
I do not have value.	I am valued.
I wasn't invited to the party because they think I am weird.	Maybe they could only have 3 friends to the party.
I will never get picked.	Sometimes I am chosen for a team.
I can keep trying my best.	I should stop trying.
It is okay to do my best at school even if my grades are not A's and B's.	I must get all A's.
I have strengths in different areas.	I screw up on everything I try. Sometimes I do better than other times.
I never do anything right without someone helping me.	I did it myself.

My life is a total mess.	There are things in my life that are positive.
I want what I want.	I am content with what I have.
It is not my fault.	Everything is my fault.
I want to get my anger out.	I just want to play.
I am a chicken.	I can listen to my feelings. Fear tells me that I may not be safe.
This is not going to ruin my whole day.	I can't do anything myself.
I can do this.	I can try.
I don't do anything right.	I am no good at school.
I am good at sports.	I am good at math.
I am a good reader.	I try my best.
I try my hardest.	I can do this.
Nobody likes me.	I have a good friend.
Some people like me.	I bet nobody will come to my party.
I bet they won't remember my birthday.	Everyone has to like me for me to feel okay.
He should share his toys with me.	I don't have to always get what I want.
I wish I were dead.	Things will get better.
I have reasons to live.	My family has a safety plan for crises.
Someone may break in.	This is stupid.
There is a light at the end of the tunnel.	My house is safe.

Figure 17: Thoughts Therapists may choose to write the following thoughts on Yellow Octagons. Additional thoughts can be added as needed. Thoughts related to peer conflict/bullying:

I think he/she will be mean to me.	I deserve to be in a safe place.
I think he/she will hit me.	I wish she/he would like me but if she/he doesn't I can accept it.
I don't want him/her to like me.	I need her/him to like me.
This person makes me uncomfortable.	He/She is in my bubble.
I can set boundaries and tell her/him that she/he is in my personal bubble.	I can walk away.
I wish they would shut up.	I can ignore them.

Figure 18: Thoughts Therapists may choose to write the following thoughts on Yellow Octagons. Additional thoughts can be added as needed. Thoughts related to attachment:

I wonder if my birth mom will come back.	I hate my dad.
My birth mom did not take care of me.	I hate my mom.
I trust my parents.	I hate my birth parents.
I am in danger.	I am safe now.
I feel unsafe.	I am safe.
I am not safe.	I do not trust my mom.
I miss my mom.	I miss my birth dad.
I miss my dad.	I miss my birth mom.
I love my dad.	I love my mom.
I am alone.	My birth family is forever.
My birth parents must not have loved me.	I wish my birth dad were here.
I won't get to eat.	My parents give me what I need.
My adoptive parents will take care of it.	My family takes care of me.
I don't trust anyone.	Nobody cares about me.
My birth parents did not care about me.	My adoptive parents will give up.
My adoptive parents are going to keep trying.	My adoptive parents are here for me no matter what.
I must not be a good person if my birth mom didn't take care of me.	My birth mom had a disease that kept her from taking care of me.
My adoptive parents want me.	It was not my fault that my birth mom did not take care of me.

Title: My View of the World

Treatment Theme: Interventions Related to Emotions, Thoughts, and Behaviors.

Treatment Goals:
1. Provide psychoeducation about cognitions.
2. Assess positive and negative thinking.
3. Encourage and assist the child in restructuring negative thoughts.

Treatment Modalities: Individual

Recommended Age Range: 4-12 years

Materials:
Paper or cardstock glasses (Available from Discount School Supplies)
Glasses with several different prescriptions (Optional)
Sunglasses with different colored lenses (Optional)
Reading glasses with different strengths (Optional)

Cost of Intervention: $

Discussion:
Cognitive Behavioral Play Therapy is based on the premise that one's thoughts impact mood and behavior (Knell, 1993). Cognitive Behavioral Play Therapy allows children and adolescents to begin to learn about their thoughts, feelings, and behaviors and the connection between them. Specifically, how one sees the world, others, and self, impacts his or her feelings and behaviors. CBPT concepts, including "how one sees the world" are abstract but can be adapted for use with a child by presenting them in a playful manner that allows for concrete representations of the concepts. Their negative thoughts, according to CBPT premises, impact behavior and mood (Knell, 1993). Changing cognitions can help address affective and behavioral treatment goals. The following intervention is considered a starting point for assessing and discussing thoughts with a child. The child's ability to communicate (verbally or by writing a list of characteristics) positive thoughts allows the therapist an important view of the child's thoughts about self. My View of the World also allows for a transitional object to remind the child of positive thinking out side of the therapeutic environment.

Knell, S. M. (1993). *Cognitive Behavioral Play Therapy.* Northvale, NJ: Jason Aronson, Inc.

Procedure:

A basket of reading and old prescription glasses are placed out at the beginning of the session. Most children gravitate towards them and begin to play with them. The child and therapist play as they discuss how glasses allow the person wearing them to see things differently. Sometimes things that are close seem further away or vice versa. One pair of glasses may provide a clear view and another pair, a fuzzy distorted view. Having extreme prescriptions will allow this concept to be even clearer. For example +4 and -4 lenses along with a slight and no correction allow for greater understanding. The clinician may also use colored sunglasses. The therapist may need to talk with parents about the myth that using glasses can damage a child's vision. Although extensive use of glasses that are not the correct prescription for the child may result in fatigue of the eyes, it does not cause any harm. The amount of time using different glasses is unlikely to fatigue the eyes. Having a period of play with the glasses is beneficial making the abstract concept of "changing one's view" using glasses and lenses more concrete. Although the activity may be done without playing with the glasses, the child is much more likely to enjoy and integrate the concept if allowed time to play with real glasses.

The child is given two pairs of cardstock glasses. The therapist and child talk about having different options for how they see the world. The child labels the two pairs of glasses to represent the pleasant and symptomatic moods. This may be mad/happy, sad/happy, pleasant/sad, negative/positive, irrational/rational, depressed/not depressed. The therapist compares the sad view of the world as being similar to how the glasses that are not the correct prescription. The child and therapist discuss how the child thinks when feeling sad and how he or she thinks when feeling happy. Thoughts are written on the respective pair of glasses. The therapist and child discuss how changing negative thoughts to positive ones can help change the child's mood. The child is encouraged to show the glasses to his or her parent or guardian and discuss them. A copy of the glasses may be made for the psychotherapy records while the child may take the glasses home. He or she is encouraged to use the happy glasses to think of thoughts that may increase positive feelings. The child is also asked to pay attention until the next session to which thoughts he or she has, when, and how often.

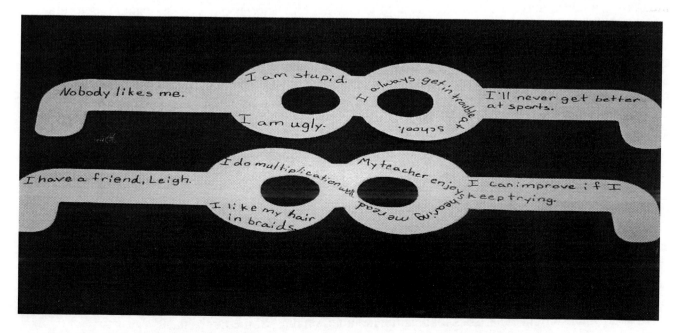

Figure 1: Two pairs of glasses with positive and negative views of self written on them.

Title: I Shine

Treatment Theme: Interventions Related to Emotions, Thoughts, and Behaviors.

Treatment Goals:
1. Assess self esteem.
2. Increase self awareness of strengths and talents.
3. Provide a concrete representation of self-esteem.
4. Decrease negative self talk and replace with positive self talk.

Treatment Modalities: Individual/Family/Group

Recommended Age Range: 5-10 years

Materials:
Cloth markers
Lamp shade
Permanent Markers

Cost of Intervention: $ to $$$
(Dependent upon whether parent is asked to supply the lamp shade)

Discussion:
Play therapists have historically been interested in self esteem as a focus of treatment. Children who present for therapy often have problems related to negative self talk and self esteem. When working with self esteem, it is important for the child to accurately self assess and develop acceptance of self. The child must be able to integrate the information, which requires time. Therefore, it is helpful to have a transitional object that helps take the concept of self esteem from therapy to the child's environment and to have the reminder over time of what characteristics he or she values about him or herself. Traditionally, Cognitive-Behavioral clinicians have rejected the concept of self esteem and it has not been considered a therapeutic focus among CBT therapists. This is due to the subjective nature of self esteem as well as the difficulty of measurement related to it. Nonetheless, as self esteem has been acknowledged as a common problem among children who present in therapy, it has become a focus of therapy among Cognitive Behavioral Therapists (Shirk, S. & Harter, S., 1996).

Shirk, S. & Harter, S. (1996). Treatment of low self-esteem. In: M.A. Reinecke, F.M. Dattillio, & A. Freeman (eds.), *Cognitive Therapy with children and adolescents: A casebook for clinical practice*. New York: Guilford Press, Inc.

Procedure:
The child and therapist discuss the child's positive attributes and abilities. The list is written on a paper. The child writes the words on the lamp shade. The child takes the lamp shade home to have a constant reminder of strengths as they "light up" his or her bedroom. The child is asked to keep track of how many times he or she notices his or her positive attributes and abilities over the next week. Homework consists of tracking this from week to week. The list that follows includes examples of positive attributes or characteristics that can be included on the I Shine lampshade.

Studious	Cute/pretty	Caring	Hard working
Intelligent	Athletic	Amiable/friendly	Ambitious
Curious	Fast	Persistent	Determined
Musical	Basketball player	Uses manners	Helpful
Great reader	Fun babysitter	Healthy eater	Inspirational
Coachable	Attentive	Focused	Obedient
Honest	Strong	Creative	Decisive
Capable	Cautious	Unique	Sensitive
Expressive	Appreciative	Imaginative	Responsible
Supportive	Artistic	Inventive	Warm
Funny	Goal-oriented	Coordinated	Active
Flexible	Organized	Neat	Logical

Title: My Crutch

Treatment Theme: Interventions Related to Emotions, Thoughts, and Behaviors

Treatment Goals:
1. Assist the child in identifying coping skills.
2. Identify coping skills as appropriate/positive or inappropriate/negative.
3. Increase the repertoire of appropriate coping skills and replace inappropriate ones.
4. Provide psychoeducation about the connection between feelings, thoughts, and behaviors.
5. Normalize responses to life events, while increasing responsibility for future behaviors.

Treatment Modalities: Individual/Family

Recommended Age Range: 6-18 years

Materials:
A crutch or assortment of crutches/canes (Often available in thrift stores)
Coach's stop watch (Optional)
Your Crutch Handout

Cost of Intervention: $$

Discussion:
Crutches are medical tools used to help with mobility when a leg is injured. Crutches help so that the person can move from place to place when they do not have use of a leg. However, the person cannot move as quickly as he or she could if they were not injured and did not need crutches. Emotional crutches, which may include negative coping skills, may get a client through a stressful time. Once a crutch is not needed it may inhibit the person from functioning optimally. Three uses of coping skills are discussed. First, coping skills may be appropriately used at appropriate times. A positive or appropriate coping skill may be talking to a trusted adult. Second, coping skills may be appropriately used at times, but only to get through a difficult time. If used beyond that time or excessively, the coping skill may become a problem instead of an aid. Sleeping may be beneficial at times but oversleeping regularly instead of facing life stressors is not helpful long-term. Third, coping skills may be inappropriate, negative behaviors, which often are used when there seemed to be no other options. Despite the behavior being inappropriate and negative, it may have been helpful for survival. An example of an inappropriate, negative coping skill is using marijuana when living in an abusive home. The negative behaviors may have been a coping skill for survival, but the behavior needs to cease for healthy living. This intervention allows the older child or adolescent to process coping skills and to determine whether they are beneficial or not. An example of an inappropriate coping skill for a younger child is hitting a sibling instead of using words.

My Crutch is a playful intervention designed to encourage developing positive, adaptive coping skills. Using My Crutch, the therapist discusses coping skills and categorizes them as appropriate/positive/ adaptive or inappropriate/negative/maladaptive. The client's coping skills are behaviors which are related to feelings and thoughts. The relationship between thinking, feeling, and behaving is processed in this intervention.

Procedure:

The concept of using a crutch is introduced. This may be done by asking questions such as whether or not the child or adolescent has ever had a broken leg and needed to use a crutch. The child is asked if he or she wants to try out some crutches. Children, and sometimes adolescents, typically enjoy trying crutches. Younger children need more concrete examples to understand the abstract concepts. However, even adults learn from the experiential portion of the activity.

The therapist has the client pretend that he or she has a broken leg that cannot be used. The therapist marks a point A and point B either in the office or, if appropriate for the therapeutic setting, in the hallway. The child tries to get from A to B with a "broken leg" which cannot be used; however, he or she is not allowed crutches. This is timed with a coach's watch. The time is written on the handout that follows. Then the child, pretending to have a broken leg and allowed to use crutches tries getting from point A to point B. This is also timed and the time is written on the form.

The child is asked to pretend that they have two healthy legs. He or she is asked to go with and without crutches from point A to B again. These are timed. The table on the handout is used to process when crutches are helpful and when they are not. Coping skills are compared to crutches. There are positive emotional crutches which are helpful to the individual. For example, using a coping skill such as talking to a friend may be like needing a crutch when one's leg is sore. Emotional crutches help the child get by or cope with a situation. In the wrong situation or continuing to use them instead of learning better coping skills, is detrimental. Some emotional crutches are almost never helpful such as using drugs or self injurious behaviors. However, even these crutches may have been helpful to temporarily cope with a stressful situation.

Examples such as the following may be given to the client.

Example 1: A child may enjoy relaxing in the tub while listening to a book on tape. He may find this comforting on a regular basis and he may seek it out when he feels sad. This is a positive coping skill.

Example 2: A child may become tearful when another child says mean things to him or her. The child seeks adult assistance in dealing with the situation. However, the child may depend on adults and not learn a more adaptive skill of being assertive. It may have been necessary to get adult assistance when the conflict started, but if the child continues to go to adults without learning to become assertive and diminish his or her dependence upon others, it becomes a crutch.

Example 3: Adolescents may use alcohol, drugs, or mild self-injurious behaviors (SIB) to cope with feelings. Drugs and SIB may dampen the pain and seem to keep the focus off the problem. However, as the adolescent uses alcohol it can become more of a problem and hinders the ability to process feelings. Although the adolescent may feel that the crutch of using alcohol or SIB was helpful at an early stage, long-term it is detrimental. As the behavior is used and the feelings are not felt, the crutch obviously becomes something that slows the person down.

My Crutch

NAME OF PLAYER	HURT WITHOUT CRUTCHES	HURT WITH CRUTCHES	NOT HURT WITHOUT CRUTCHES	NOT HURT WITH CRUTCHES

Sometimes I have unpleasant feelings or thoughts. Some unpleasant feelings include anger, sadness, and jealousy. Some unpleasant thoughts may include "I am not smart enough" or "The other girls do not like me."

When I feel _____ or think _____, sometimes I do a behavior that may at times help me cope. Some coping skills are helpful and some are harmful. Some coping skills can also be either helpful or harmful depending on the situation. If this coping skill is used too much or is used instead of learning other coping skills, which may be more helpful for me, it becomes a crutch. For example, sleeping can be helpful when feeling upset if it is used occasionally and in a situation when sleeping is acceptable. However, sleeping during school is not helpful because I cannot learn while I am asleep. If sleeping is used too often as a coping skill, it can also be hurtful.

List 5-10 coping skills that may be used when you have the above feeling or thought.

Make a smile beside each one that will likely be a helpful coping skill. Make a question mark by those that may be either helpful or a "crutch." Cross out those that are hurtful or always a crutch. Practice those that are helpful. Talk with someone you trust about when the coping skills that you labeled with a question mark may be helpful.

Coping Skills:
1.
2.
3.
4.
5.

Title: I-Feel: Assertiveness Puzzle

Treatment Theme: Interventions Related to Emotions, Thoughts, and Behaviors

Treatment Goals:
1. Encourage the child to use I-statements for assertive, respectful communication.
2. Break the I-statement into three components.
3. Assist the child in putting the three parts of the I-statement together both as a puzzle and verbally in the form of a complete I-statement.
4. Provide a means for the child to self-check whether they have used the three components of an I-statement.
5. Provide a transitional object for the child to encourage use of the technique at home or school.

Treatment Modalities: Individual/Family/Group

Recommended Age Range: 5-18 years

Materials:
I-Statement Puzzles
Blank Puzzles

Cost of Intervention: $

Discussion:
Children and adolescents often have difficulty learning to be assertive in interpersonal interactions. I-statements can be an effective strategy for clients to learn to identify what they feel and say what they would like to have change. The I-statement puzzle allows the child to think of the three important components of the I-statement.

Procedure:
When it seems that an I-statement may be beneficial for the client, the therapist may discuss the components of an I-statement with the child. The I-Feel puzzle is introduced to the child. If using the blank puzzle, the child writes the three components of an I-statement on the three puzzle pieces. The I-statement puzzle is separated into three pieces. The child and therapist take turns practicing each of the parts of an I-statement with a situation the child has been in. The child takes the I-statement puzzle home as a reminder of the technique and to utilize when doing homework related to using it when having interpersonal difficulties.

In a later session, the child writes the three components on the three segments of the puzzle. This reinforces remembering the important components of the I-statement. The client and therapist, with puppets if desired, use role plays of situations when I-statements may be helpful.

I-Statement Puzzle Template: Client adds steps of I-Statements.

I feel _____.
When you _____.
I wish you would _____.

I-Statement Puzzle Template: Steps of I-Statements included.

I feel _____

when you _____

I wish you would _____.

Title: Create your Future: Anti-Fortune Teller

Treatment Theme: Interventions Related to Emotions, Thoughts, and Behaviors

Treatment Goals:
1. Discuss the child's ability to actively make changes.
2. Increase the child's feelings of mastery, self-sufficiency, and hope.
3. List and practice coping skills that will increase the child's ability to decrease presenting problems.
4. Create a transitional object the child may take home that allows for review of coping skills.

Treatment Modalities: Individual/Group

Recommended Age Range: 8-12 years

Materials:
Fortune teller directions for cutting and folding
Pens or other writing utensils
List of coping skills/behaviors consistent with client's presenting problem

Cost of Intervention: $

Advanced Preparation:
Cut a Fortune Teller from paper using the template below. Write names of colors such as Red, Green, Blue, and Purple on the outside of the Fortune Teller colors. On the inside flaps, eight numbers are written. On the inside of the most interior flap, positive behaviors or coping skills are written on the inside.

Discussion:
Young adolescents and pre-teens have enjoyed fortune tellers for generations. They are an engaging and familiar way to present options. Crisci, Lay, and Lowenstein utilized a fortune teller in an engaging intervention for sexually abused children (1996). However, the intent with this intervention is not only to engage the child but also encourage an active role in changing one's own life. It is therapeutic for the client to learn that he or she has control over some aspects of his or her life. This is the message communicated when playing the Create your Future Anti-Fortune Teller Game.

Crisci, G., Lay, M., & Lowenstein, L. (1998). *Paper dolls and paper airplanes: Therapeutic exercises for sexually traumatized children*. Indianapolis: Kidsrights.

Procedure:
The therapist discusses with the child, his or her ability to make changes in his or her life. The Fortune Teller allows for a discussion about whether the child has control of his or her own life as opposed to feeling helpless, and without power to change things in his or her life. The following discussion is an example of what the therapist and older client may discuss.

"In therapy we discuss things that you can change. A Fortune Teller is a fun game where you are told what will happen to you in the future. Often we can make choices or behave in certain ways to create our futures. We are in charge of our futures. Instead of having fortunes read to you with this game, we will read statements about what you can do to make your life more like what you want it to be."

1. Fold a square sheet of paper into a triangle. (If the paper is not square, cut it so that it is.)

2. Fold the opposite ends of the triangle together. This will result in a smaller triangle.

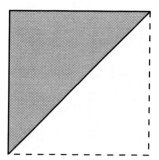

3. Open the paper by unfolding all the folds. The paper will be a square with bends making four equal triangles.

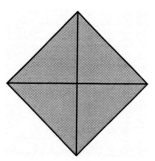

4. Fold a corner in so that the point touches the center.

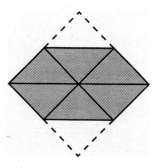

5. Repeat with all four corners so that a square is created.

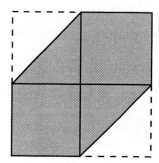

6. Turn the paper to the other side. Fold all four corners to the center. This will create a small square.

7. Fold the square in half, creating a long rectangle. Unfold so that you have a square again. Then fold the other way and unfold.

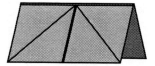

8. Unfold, and then put your fingers into the holes. Mold with your fingers so that it feels comfortable and moves easily.

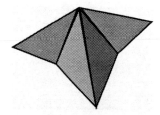

9. Write colors on the flaps.

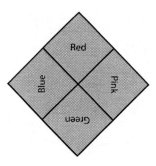

10. Write numbers 1-8 on the triangular flaps on the other side.

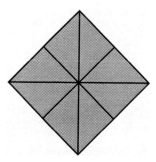

11. Write Anti-Fortunes underneath the numbers. The positive coping skills listed below are categorized according to presenting problem. Examples are given on the pages that follow. The suggestions may be used or create individualized Anti-Fortunes with the client that relate directly to his or her situations.

12. The child's or therapist's index finger and thumb from each hand are placed into the flaps. The fingers go into the bottom of the Anti-Fortune Teller so that when the fingers are mold into it, the colors are seen from the top. The Anti-Fortune Teller is molded to the fingers so that it is flexible moving back and forth. The fingers are pinched together alternating between pushing together and pulling back.

Playing the Anti-Fortune Teller:

1. Have the child pick a color for those listed on the Anti-Fortune Teller. Move it back and forth as the color is spelled out. For example, if the color is red, the Anti-Fortune Teller is moved three times as the color R-E-D is spelled out.

2. The child then picks a number from those seen inside the Anti-Fortune Teller and the Anti-Fortune Teller is moved back and forth as the number is counted out. For example, the number three is counted out 1-2-3 while the Anti-Fortune Teller is pinched and pulled back and forth.

3. Repeat step 2 with the child choosing another visible number.

4. Lift the flap and read the positive statement or coping skill. Process the statement and discuss how it may help.

5. Send the Anti-Fortune Teller home with the client as a transition object and to emphasize the concept of taking control of the aspects he or she can control.

6. Use the Anti-Fortune Teller at the beginning or end of sessions to remind the client of positive coping skills.

Anti-Fortune Teller Statements for Depression:

You will feel less sad as you do more fun activities. List three fun things you can do.

You can decide how to think about your situation. Name one thought that you have that could make you feel sad. What might you think instead?

You can find someone who will listen when you need someone to talk to. Who is one person you trust?

Healthy habits help make kids feel better. Name one thing you can do to improve your sleep.

You are talented. Name one thing you do well.

You can create happy moments by making changes in your life. What changes can you make today to make your life better?

You can have rewarding friendships. What are five things you do to make your friendships stronger?

Try again when at first you do not succeed. What does this mean and how does it apply to you?

If you were to receive an award what would it be? How can you mark your accomplishments yourself?

Your problems will get easier when you learn 4 coping skills. Name 4 coping skills you have worked on.

You deserve time to relax. What are two things you like to do to relax? How often do you do them?

Anti-Fortune Teller Statements for Anxiety:

Having support to deal with anxiety can be helpful. Who are three of your strongest supporters?

Three distraction activities are doing a word puzzle, watching TV and talking to a friend. Which would you choose?

Knowing that you feel anxious is the first step to dealing with anxiety. How do you know when you are anxious?

Facing anxiety is helpful in learning to overcome anxiety. What motivates you to face it?

Distraction can be helpful at times when dealing with anxiety. When have you found distraction useful?

What are five distraction activities that you have found useful?

Anxiety may decrease when you use relaxation. Name a relaxation activity you use.

You deserve time to relax. What are two things you like to do to relax? How often do you do them?

Anti-Fortune Teller Statements for Girls' Friendships/Social issues:

Ask an acquaintance to go for ice cream or a movie.

Ask questions about another girl's interests to get to know more about her. Use What, Why, Where, When, Who, and How questions.

People value many things in friends such as honesty or a sense of humor.
What are three things you value in a friend?

People can think differently and still be friends. What is one thing you and a friend think differently about?

Friends communicate in many ways. They text, talk, and use body language. What are your favorite ways to communicate?

Often girls like to be friends with others who have similar interests. What are three topics, sports or musical groups that interest you?

Family members can make good friends. Are you friends with family members? Who?

Title: It's a Puzzle: Problem Solving Puzzle

Treatment Theme: Interventions Related to Emotions, Thoughts, and Behaviors

Treatment Goals:
1. Teach steps of problem solving.
2. Provide a concrete representation of how each step is necessary to solve problems optimally.
3. Provide a transitional object that can be used when problem solving at home or school.

Treatment Modalities: Individual

Recommended Age Range: 4-14 years

Advanced Preparation:
The puzzle pieces can be photocopied onto paper or cardstock and laminated if desired. Laminating may be beneficial for generalizing the behavior to the home or school environment as the puzzle will last longer.

Materials:
Puzzle with or without steps written on the pieces

Cost of Intervention: $

Discussion:
Problem solving is an important therapeutic skill for several clinical child and adolescent populations. For example, depressed adolescents have been found to be lacking problem solving skills (Adams & Adams, 1991). For children who have been traumatized, problem solving offers empowerment and mastery through learning to make changes in areas of their lives where change is possible. Children with behavioral problems, such as those with ODD or ADHD, benefit from problem solving by learning adaptive ways to cope with problems or conflicts.

Problem solving is important for helping children make changes. Stark et. al., (2006) discusses the problem solving steps involved in the Cognitive Behavioral Treatment of depression. The problem solving steps consist of problem definition, goal definition, solution generation, consequential thinking, and self-evaluation. The It's a Puzzle intervention uses problem solving steps in a manner which allows the child to engage in play increasing the likelihood that the child will be engaged in the process.

The following intervention includes problem solving steps discussed in the literature in a manner that allows for generalization of the skill and playfulness of the intervention. Generalization of the skill is important as literature suggests that some children, such as children with ADHD, do not use problem solving skills outside of the environment in which the skill is taught (Hinshaw & Erhardt, 1991). The puzzle also emphasizes that each piece is necessary, but not sufficient for problem solving with a self-correcting quality.

Adams, M. & Adams, J. (1991). *Life events, depression, and perceived problem solving alternatives in adolescents*. Journal of Child Psychology and Psychiatry, 32, 811-820.

Hirshaw, S.P., & Erhardt, D. (1991). Attention-deficit hyperactivity disorder. In: P.C. Kendall (Ed.), *Child and adolescent behavior therapy: Cognitive-behavioral procedures* (pp. 98-130). New York: Guilford Press.

Stark, K.D., Hargrave, J., Sander, J., Custer, G., Schnoebelen, S., Simpson, J., & Molnar, J. (2006). Treatment of childhood depression: The ACTION treatment program. In: P.C. Kendall (Ed.), *Child and adolescent therapy: Cognitive behavioral procedures.* (p. 182) New York: Guilford Press.

Procedure:

The therapist discusses problem solving with the child. The reasons why a child may want to use problem solving are articulated. Common cognitive and environmental reasons for resistance to problem solving are discussed. For example, for children with depression, problem solving may be difficult since the child may expect negative outcomes. Therefore, the child with depression may feel that using problem solving will not help.

The steps of problem solving are discussed. The therapist indicates that the steps can be considered pieces of a puzzle. It is noted that the client needs all the pieces of the puzzle to successfully problem solve. The therapist may use the puzzles with the steps on them. Alternatively, blank puzzles are also included. The child or adolescent writes the steps on the blank puzzle. The puzzle is taken apart and a common problem is discussed. For each problem solving step that is applied to that problem, the corresponding piece is put together. This proceeds until the puzzle is complete. The therapist and child decide on a problem in the child's life, typically a small, manageable problem, to use the problem solving procedure. The puzzle is sent with the child with homework related to a specific problem to work on before the next session.

Problem solving instructions that the client may write on the puzzle follow.

Problem Solving for Younger Children
1. What is the problem?
2. What are three things you could do to change it?
3. Try one.
4. How did it work?
5. If it worked well, celebrate.
6. If it did not work well, try another.

Problem Solving for Older Children and Adolescents
1. What is the problem?
2. How would you like it to be?
3. What are possible options to cope with or change the problem?
4. Pick one of the options.
5. Use the option.
6. Decide if the option worked. How well did it work?
7. Decide whether a different option would have worked better.
8. Try another option if needed.

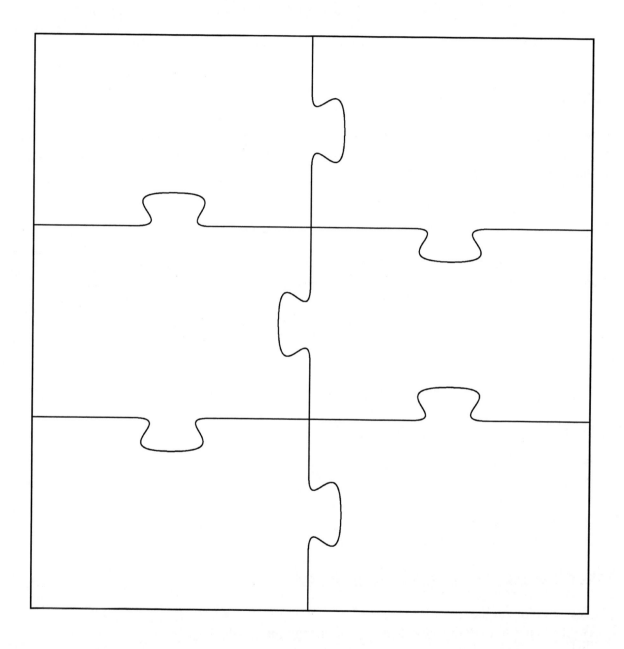

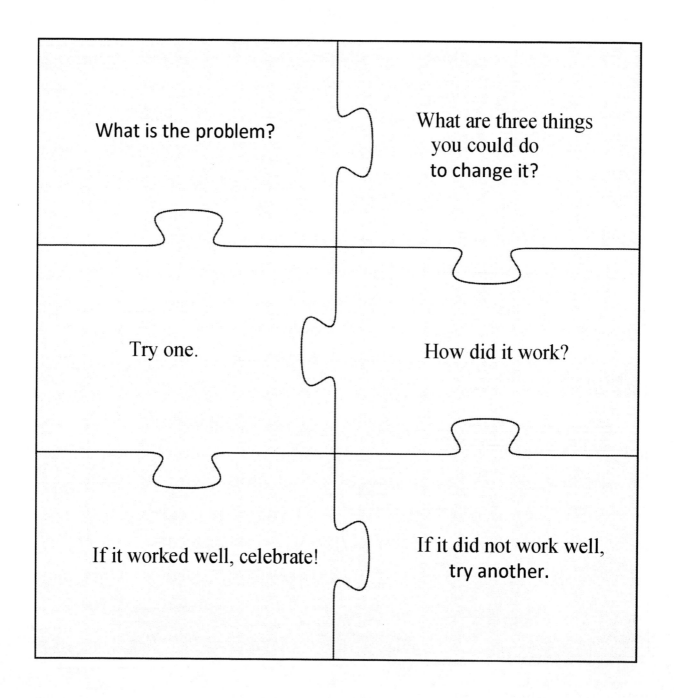

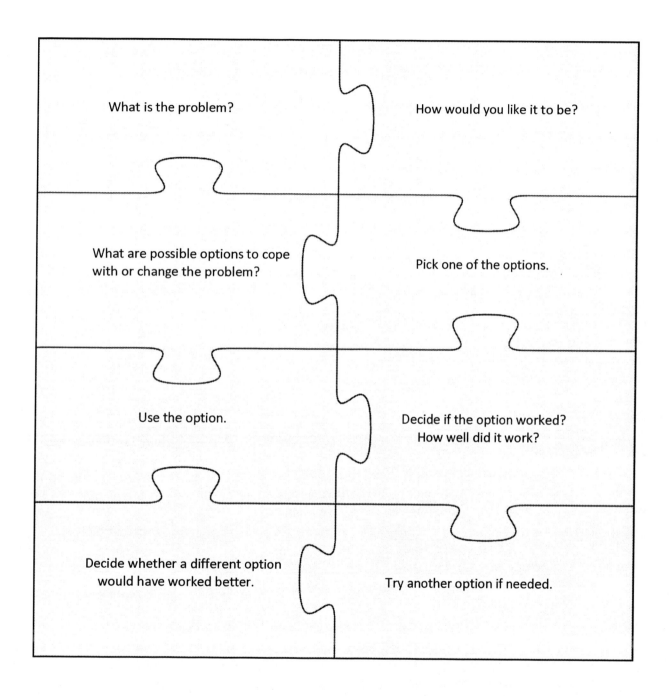

What is the problem?

How would you like it to be?

What are possible options to cope with or change the problem?

Pick one of the options.

Use the option.

Decide if the option worked? How well did it work?

Decide whether a different option would have worked better.

Try another option if needed.

Title: Counting Sheep Pillowcase: Strategies for Improving Sleep

Treatment Theme: Interventions Related to Emotions, Thoughts, and Behaviors

Treatment Goals:
1. Introduce the concept of behavioral changes that could improve sleep (Sleep Hygiene).
2. Provide a transitional object that reminds the child and parent of tips for sleep hygiene.
3. Engage the child in changing behaviors around bedtime routine.

Treatment Modalities: Individual/Family/Group

Recommended Age Range: 3-12 years

Materials:
Pillowcase (Available through Discount School Supplies)
Permanent markers or fabric paints
List of sleep hygiene strategies

Cost of Intervention: $

Discussion:
Often children with emotional and behavioral problems have difficulty with sleep. This intervention allows the therapist to provide suggestions for improving sleep in a format that will be more likely to be helpful to the child and parent than a discussion or even a list written on paper. The child is typically engaged in the process by writing or illustrating the recommendations.

Procedure:
The child, parent, and therapist discuss specific problems related to sleep as well as the child's bedtime routines. The therapist gets a history of factors related to the child's sleep problems. The history taking may be done while acting out the bedtime practices in the dollhouse for a 5-10 year old child as this may help them think about the nighttime rituals. The therapist and child talk about things that the child could do to improve sleep. The following is a list of options:

- Keep your eyes closed when trying to fall asleep.
- No talking when trying to fall asleep.
- No moving (children sometimes move each time they start to relax and keep themselves from falling asleep).
- No electronics (TV, Computer, Videogames) for 2-3 hours before bedtime.
- No electronics in children's bedrooms.
- No caffeine after 2 pm (Drink only beverages that do not have caffeine).
- Keep bedtime calm and relaxed.
- Have a bedtime routine.

The child draws or writes the sleep hygiene factors on a pillow case. The pillow case is taken home where it is available at bedtime as a reminder of the interventions that may help.

Title: Right Address/Wrong Address: Messages from Self and Others

Treatment Theme: Interventions Related to Emotions, Thoughts, and Behaviors

Treatment Goals:
1. Process rational (positive) and irrational (negative) thoughts.
2. Provide a concrete example of the abstract concept of accepting or rejecting thoughts.
3. Confront negative thoughts related to the self and increase the positive view of self.

Treatment Modalities: Individual

Recommended Age Range: 4-12 years

Materials:
Two cardstock mailboxes or shoe boxes
Paper for writing letters/notes to self
Pencil, pen, colored pencils, markers or crayons
Postal worker dress up clothes (Optional)
Postal worker bag (Optional)
Homemade or purchased greeting cards related to several occasions and several related to inspiration and appreciation towards the receiver. (Optional)

Cost of Intervention: $

Advanced Preparation:
Two mailboxes are made using cardstock mailboxes or empty boxes such as shoe boxes. Cardstock mailboxes are typically available around Valentine's Day in the arts and crafts section or close to the cards used for classroom exchange. The mailboxes can be decorated; the Right Address mailbox can be decorated with symbols of hope and happiness and the Wrong Address mailbox with symbols of sadness or worry. Making mailboxes from boxes such as shoe boxes can also be given homework for children who are likely to do homework

Discussion:
The child and therapist address messages that the child sends to herself. For young children 4-8 it is essential that the abstract concept of self-statements or positive or negative thoughts about self, others, and the world is made concrete. This exercise allows for an engaging intervention that addresses this concept.

Procedure:
Optional play for initial engagement in the activity: With younger children, the Right Address/Wrong Address intervention can be started by playing postal carrier with the child. This can include dressing up in the postal worker uniform. The child is offered a bag which can be used to deliver letters. The child is shown a mailbox into which letters can be placed. The child and therapist can also be engaged by reading letters from the mailboxes. Assorted cards for different occasions may be available for the child to use. This play is beneficial in engaging the child in the activity.

The child and therapist then talk about how messages are given to a child in many ways. The most obvious way is to receive a letter. Examples are given such "When Grandma sends a letter saying 'Happy Birthday', how does that make you feel? What is the message that she is sending?" Explain to the child that part of the message is written and part is inferred. Both the literal and inferred messages are processed. The therapist (or the child) writes the messages down on post cards. The messages are placed into the Right Address or Wrong Address mailbox. Several examples of messages that the child has received are discussed. Messages may be given to the child based on things a person says to the child, or things that the person does to or for the child. For children who have been abused or neglected, the behaviors that the parent had are discussed related to the messages that the child was given. Messages that are not helpful are placed into the Wrong Address mailbox; those that are helpful are placed into the Right Address mailbox.

The child also processes messages that he or she gives to him or herself. Messages to the self are described to the child as things that the child thinks about himself. This may need to be described as the words that you say to yourself about yourself. The messages that the child has about him or herself are often reflections of messages from early caregiving. Examples may need to be given. It is very helpful to have a list of statements the child has made in recent sessions about him or herself. The statements can be written on "letters" or "messages" as specific examples. The child is asked to write several short letters or messages to him or herself on postcards. The therapist can assist with the letters either playing the secretary by dictating the letter, or by giving some short letter fragments. The more information directly given by the child, the more effective the intervention can be. However, it may be necessary to give some guidance in the writing. Common thinking errors in the messages that a child may give to him or herself may be compared to address mistakes.

For older children, thinking errors may be related to the address metaphor used in the Right Address/Wrong Address play. The child and therapist may construct a list of reasons that messages are sent to the wrong address and do not have to be accepted in the child's mailbox. For example, when the child has thoughts that are very extreme such as "I never make good choices" the therapist can talk about how that message should be addressed to the south pole because it is so extreme just like the south pole is an extreme place— far from everything and with an extreme temperature. The child's extreme messages can be placed in the Wrong Address mailbox. The therapist or child may write South Pole on the postcard on which the message is written. In future sessions the therapist may continue to refer to any extreme statements as being letters that should be sent to the South Pole.

Messages that contain names such as "stupid" or "ugly" or other negative names can be described as being sent to the wrong person. The therapist can help the child think about how to confront the name calling such as writing in bold letters across the postcard "NO SUCH PERSON AT THIS ADDRESS." The therapist and child then talk about not accepting messages that are not accurate about themselves from self or others.

When messages contain words such as "never" or "always" the child and therapist can decide the messages are not coming to the right address. These may include extreme messages, name calling or labeling, emotional responding (seeing things as all bad when feeling depressed), predictions. Messages that predict what will happen and do so in a negative way are sent to the Wrong Address mailbox.

Another cognitive distortion is addressed when noting that emotions change the view of the message. When a message focuses on negative feelings, it is easy to see the situation as bad and this makes the person feel even worse; when this type of message is sent to the child he or she may reject it as it was sent to the wrong address.

When messages that contain a negative message are inflated, the message may be written on a very big piece of paper. That the message is inflated, not accurate is noted as the therapist indicates that the message was sent to the wrong address.

The child may also receive messages that have errors because the sender of the message is wrong. Messages related to abuse, for example, contain information that the child can reject. The therapist and child may practice writing RETURN TO SENDER on messages that contain abuse-related messages that are not accurate.

Using this playful metaphor, the child is helped to look at messages (cognitive distortions) and practice rejecting the message. These messages, that reflect cognitive distortions, do not need to be accepted. The child may rewrite the messages to be more accurate. The child may decide to place them in the Wrong Address mailbox. Messages are collected from the mailboxes and may be photocopied for the therapeutic record. They may be kept across sessions to readdress the messages in this playful metaphor in a later session.

Melissa and Doug Mailbox Alternative to the Right Address/Wrong Address intervention:
An alternative is to use a children's toy mailbox such as the one available from Melissa and Doug. Although this is an expensive alternative, it is sturdy and can endure years of multiple clients' use. Two adhesive hooks are attached to the inside of the mailbox by the opening of each slot. A bag is attached to the hooks and positioned so that the "mail" can be placed into the bag from the slot. The Melissa and Doug mailbox has three slots. Therefore, there are two slots to hold messages that are to the Right Address and one to the Wrong Address.

Interventions
for
Processing
Trauma

Title: Nested Boxes: Building Coping Skills Prior to Processing Trauma

Treatment Theme: Interventions for Processing Trauma

Treatment Goals:
1. Provide psychoeducation about the progressive steps in therapy to gain skills that are necessary prior to addressing the trauma.
2. Provide the child with a visual, concrete representation of the abstract concept of the progressive steps in trauma treatment.
3. Provide a concrete example of containment of the trauma.

Treatment Modalities: Individual/Family/Group

Recommended Age Range: 5-18 years

Materials:
5 nested boxes (Available at craft stores)
Markers/colored pencils/crayons
Paper

Cost of Intervention: $

Discussion:
At the beginning of therapy with traumatized children, it is beneficial to discuss the treatment plan with the client and parents. If the child is going to discuss and process traumatic events, it is especially important that they be prepared for this important and therapeutically powerful step. Clients are prepared to discuss and process trauma through therapeutic goals met earlier in the therapy. For example, the child must learn about feelings and coping skills before discussing his or her trauma narrative.

Once the skills are developed, the child's processing of the narrative is more likely to be beneficial since the skills will facilitate healing. Children and adolescents who have been traumatized often have questions about treatment. Some have an especially difficult time with the concept of discussing the trauma or being exposed to stimuli that remind them of the trauma. Some children or their parents/guardians may decide to discontinue with therapy if they feel processing the traumatic events will be detrimental to the child. Other children want to jump to discussing the traumatic event early in treatment. When the child does not have sufficient resources internally or externally to cope with the processing of trauma, it can be detrimental to proceed with discussion of the trauma too soon.

The Nested Boxes intervention allows the therapist to make the steps of therapy concrete. It allows the child to understand the steps that literature and research indicate are important to work on before the trauma is discussed. It allows the child to understand that although the clinician feels that processing the trauma is essential for the therapy outcome, it can only be done after the client has learned skills to cope with the trauma and heal from processing it. The child learns that the trauma is contained and later "taken out" and addressed after the earlier skills are learned. This provides the child with safety and security prior to the describing of the traumas and the processing of the narrative.

This intervention is most applicable to Trauma Focused-Cognitive Behavioral Therapy (TF-CBT) for traumatized children, though it can be utilized with other models of treatment of childhood trauma. The components of TF-CBT are: Psychoeducation, Parenting skills, Relaxation, Affective modulation, Cognitive coping/processing, Trauma narrative, In vivo mastery, Conjoint child-parent sessions, and Enhancing future safety (Cohen, Mannarino, Deblinger, 2006). Each of the components has been supported by research as essential for progress in reducing symptoms. The components of TF-CBT have been combined into five groups of therapeutic concepts. The five groups are explained to children in a simple manner with the Nested Boxes intervention.

Cohen, J., Mannarino, A., & Deblinger, E. (2006). *Treating trauma and traumatic grief in children and adolescents.* New York: Guilford Press.

Procedure:

The therapist and traumatized child discuss the treatment plan and the steps that will be taken to meet treatment goals. The therapist tells the child about the importance of talking about the trauma. The child and parent are told that many coping skills are developed before the trauma is processed. Then they are told of the process and how they will be supported in the process.

The therapist describes the components of therapy that will addressed prior to discussing the trauma. Nested boxes are presented to the child. The Nested Boxes depict stages of therapy. The outer-most box depicts the earliest stage of therapy.

The outer most box may be summarized as "Helping Families." The important concepts of helping families may include the following:

- Teaching parents about praise and reinforcement
- Teaching parents to set limits
- Teaching parents and kids about how people, including kids, react to trauma
- Talking about ways to stay safe in the future.

The next box is described as "Learning about Feelings." The important components of "Learning about Feelings" include:
- Identifying feelings in yourself and others
- What happens inside bodies when you have different feelings?
- What do faces and bodies look like when someone has a certain feeling?

The next box is "Teaching Children to Relax" which includes:
- Distraction
- Relaxation
- Imagery
- Mindfulness.

The next box is titled "The Cognitive Triangle: How Feelings, Thoughts, and Behaviors Influence Each Other" which include the following concepts:
- Ways to change feelings and behaviors
- Thought stopping and other cool ways to deal with feelings.

The inner most box is titled:
- "The Thing that Happened and Remembering and Dealing with it."

The child then decorates each box with symbols that represent the step the box represents. For example, the child draws faces on a box representing learning about feelings. Inside each box the child places the smaller boxes.

During the process of therapy, the child and therapist bring the nested boxes out to discuss their progress towards therapeutic goals. As the goals of each of the components are met, the box is filled with slips of paper with concrete skills that were met with the respective goal. For example, the coping skills related to feelings identification are written on slips of paper. These may include such things as:
- Learned about 15 different feelings.
- Learned about levels of anger (annoyed, angry, rage).

As therapy progresses, the child will meet goals related to each of the outer boxes. By the time the child has learned the skills necessary to successfully process the narrative; the child can see a concrete representation of why the therapist feels he or she is ready to process the narrative. When a child wants to process the narrative before the necessary coping skills are in place, the therapist may use the Nested Boxes as a visual to help explain why the child will be more prepared to share the narrative after learning other skills, such as affect modulation, which will be helpful when the narrative is shared. If there is hesitation in the child or parent, the nested boxes are referenced to show that the foundation has been laid. As the coping skills are needed during the processing of the narrative, the therapist can review the coping skills from earlier boxes as he or she suggests using them.

Title: Pffft-That's Just What Bodies Do: Normalizing Sexual Responses in Children Who Have Been Sexually Abused.

Treatment Theme: Interventions for Processing Trauma

Recommended Age Range: 5 to 18 years (Adapted to the child)

Treatment Modality: Individual/Family/Group

Goals:
1. Provide psychoeducation about physiological responses to sexual abuse.
2. Reduce feelings of shame about having a physiological response to sexual abuse.
3. Provide a mature defense mechanism (humor) to an experience that previously may have elicited immature defenses and feelings of shame.
4. Provide an opportunity for the child to feel empowered by understanding normal bodily functions and responses.
5. Discuss when behaviors are acceptable (discussion about body functions) and when it's better to wait to discuss them.

Materials: Whoopee Cushions

Cost of Intervention: $

Discussion:
When children are sexually abused, they sometimes have a physiological reaction such as having an erection or orgasm. Often this produces feelings of shame and guilt and questions about whether they enjoyed the sexual abuse or even if they were responsible for it. This intervention was developed when searching for a lecture-free method that would be unlikely to elicit shame from children who experienced some pleasurable feelings during sexual abuse. Often children will restrict talk about physiological responses. This may be due to fear that others will feel that they made the abuse happen. This intervention frees children to process the feelings about the physiological response (i.e., enjoyable, uncomfortable, painful).

Clinical judgment should be used to decide whether a child would be able to discuss this topic in this way. Thoughts of one's body responding to abuse can elicit feelings of shame and guilt, so it is important to implement it after having strong rapport. It is also important to have the intervention followed by calming activities (i.e., breathing exercises) and activities that provide the client with refocusing on the here and now. If a child seems highly anxious, this intervention may need to wait. If court is likely, it may be advisable to utilize this intervention after court.

This intervention should be used with discretion when the non-offending parent is not supportive or feels the child is partially responsible. If the unsupportive non-offending parent feels the child has enjoyed or reacted to the abuse, they may feel the child is responsible. Clinical judgment should guide whether the intervention will educate the parent or provide information that allows for further blame of the victim.

This can be a powerful group exercise; however, it is most effective when the group is small and a high level of trust has been established within the group. Group members should be allowed discretion in deciding whether or not to share their responses with the group.

Description:

The clinician may start the technique by sitting on a whoopee cushion and letting the child hear it. Typically, this results in hesitant snickers followed by laughter. The child then uses the whoopee cushion. The child and therapist can enjoy each other and compete in contests to see who can make certain sounds (i.e., the loudest or softest).

After playing with the whoopee cushion, the clinician changes the tone to that of psychoeducation. Psychoeducation begins with a brief description of different normal physiological responses (tears when exposed to onion, mucus produced in the nose, kicking when tapped with the mallet at the doctor's office, wax produced in ears). The therapist may give examples of times when someone had had a normal physiological response and felt feelings of shame or embarrassment.

The therapist can provide the child with psychoeducation related to physiological responses when sexually touched. Psychoeducation includes the fact that sexual touch, even during abuse, may feel good to the child and this does not make it the child's fault. The therapist may be specific about common physiological responses especially when the child has indicated that he or she had them. If the child has brought up physiological reactions in past sessions, he or she can discuss it further with this intervention. Often this activity allows the child to discuss previously unspoken aspects of their abuse. The child is also more likely to ask questions that may have been confusing or shameful. For example, a child who had an orgasm may be ashamed to talk about the sensations and may not have asked an adult about the experience which he or she did not understand.

During this activity, it is important to discuss socially appropriate behaviors. While the therapy session provides an environment where the client can discuss difficult topics, socially appropriate boundaries must be discussed. For example, it is socially inappropriate to make the sounds in some places (i.e., the classroom). The specifics about when it is appropriate to talk about body functions are discussed.

Title: The Spider and The Fly: Bibliotherapy for Understanding Perpetrators

Treatment Theme: Interventions for Processing Trauma

Treatment Goals:
1. Address cognitive distortions related to victims and offenders of abuse.
2. Playfully explore the power differential between victims and offenders.
3. Provide psychoeducation related to safety issues specifically related to interpersonal violence.
4. Encourage identification with empowered survivors of interpersonal offenses.

Treatment Modalities: Individual/Family/Group

Recommended Age Range: 12-18 years

Materials:
DiTerlizzi, T. (2002). *The spider and the fly.* New York: Simon & Schuster Books.

Cost of Intervention: $

Discussion:
This intervention is intended for older children and adolescents who struggle with co-dependent relationships and being victimized. It is especially helpful when processing the grooming process of sexual abuse or the honeymoon stage with interpersonal violence. Often adolescents enjoy reading a book written for younger children in session. It provides a nurturing activity and emotional distance while processing abuse.

Procedure:
The therapist and client read the book *The Spider and the Fly* together. The therapist uses clinical discretion to decide whether to process the book during or after reading the book. The therapist and client stay within the metaphor of the book initially and move towards the client's individual issues as they pertain to the perpetrator or the victim in the story.

Processing Questions: The Spider and the Fly Intervention

How does the spider decide what comments will work to trick the fly?

Why does the spider keep commenting when the fly rejects his comments?

Do you think the fly could get the comments from another less dangerous insect suitor?

Does the spider speak the truth or does the spider say what the fly wants to hear? Could it be both? Does he exaggerate the truth? Does he believe what he says?

How could the fly accept that she has a need to have others appreciate her but not become a target of someone who is not sincere?

Does having the need to hear nice things about her mean something negative about the fly?

Why was the spider so patient?

What clues does the fly see that the spider is not genuine? Why does she ignore them?

Does the spider see the fly as a beautiful fly or a delicious meal?

How does the fly's training in being polite make her more vulnerable?

Why does the fly keep coming back? Does the spider know the fly will return? Does he care whether it is this particular fly or any other fly?

What could an older, wiser mentor tell the fly to keep her from getting captured? Would she listen to the advice? Why?

If she would have escaped, what might she use to teach other flies how to keep from being caught by this or other spiders?

Whose fault was it that the fly was caught? Is it possible to help the fly become safer in the future by changing her behavior without blaming her victimization on herself? (It was not her fault. It was the spider's fault. However, she could have made decisions that would have kept her safe.)

Do you think that the spider enjoyed this process? Was it part of the game?

What would a 'spider' use to seduce you?

What sticky web would a spider catch you in? What words could be used to make the web in which you would be caught?

Title: Quilt to Safety/Dreidels for Coping: Embracing Cultural Legacies of Survival

Treatment Theme: Interventions for Processing Trauma

Treatment Goals:
1. Provide contemporary and historical examples of those who have survived abuses.
2. Provide personal and group examples of finding ways to survive.
3. Encourage identification with survival and empowerment.

Treatment Modalities: Individual/Family/Group

Recommended Age Range: 8-18 years

Materials:
Books such as:
Levine, E. (2007). *Henry's Freedom Box: A true story from the Underground Railroad*. New York: Scholastic Press.

Hopkinson, D. (1993). *Sweet Clara and the freedom quilt*. New York: Dragonfly books.

Woodson, J. (2005). *Show way*. New York: G.P. Putnam's Sons.

Cost of Intervention: $

Discussion:
Identification with other survivors can be beneficial to the client. Often this is a connection formed with other members of a support group or peers with whom they discover shared experiences. At times, especially for older children and adolescents, it may be helpful to connect the client to the shared experience of survival from maltreatment and claiming survivor status. It can be helpful to find survivors who are role models of a similar background such as race or gender. However, identification as a survivor could also include learning from those of different backgrounds. Having several examples can be helpful.

Across cultures, people who have been oppressed or abused have found ways to survive. This intervention allows for the treatment team to provide stories that celebrate the survival of oppressed and abused groups. These can include children who have been sexually abused or cultures who have suffered persecution. The stories allow for survivor identification and feelings of empowerment. A survivor's quilt, is a visual of the child's own survival and a transitional object following the session.

Bibliotherapy or oral storytelling is helpful in psychoeducation related to being a survivor. The therapist reads a book to the client about a survivor. Even older children and adolescents often respond well to having a meaningful book read during a session for bibliotherapy. One important story of survival was that of the slaves. The books referenced above, *Show Way* or *Sweet Clara and the Freedom Quilt,* can be beneficial in introducing the story. Both books tell the story of slaves escaping from the southern United States by using quilts. The quilts were maps made to represent the routes to freedom. The quilts provided safety, such as those affiliated with the Underground Railroad, were marked. This intervention addresses the similarity of survivors of abuses. Each survivor has his or her own survival story and his or her own path from abuse to safety. This intervention is a visual reminder and celebration of the client's path.

Another survival story is that of the Jewish people during Roman rule. A short version of the story follows: Jewish people during the Bar Kokhba revolution were oppressed and their religion was made illegal (Kimmel, 1998). Surviving includes spiritual survival, the ability to practice one's religion. The Jewish people needed to meet and discuss the Torah and how to survive their oppression. However, the Roman soldiers traveled from house to house, looking for people who were studying the Torah. The people played a common game, dreidels, during their meetings. When Romans came to the get-togethers, and saw them playing this was considered an acceptable activity. However, it was much more than just a game; it was a coping skill used to survive and trick the Romans. People use different things to survive oppression and abuse. Survival is on different levels; physically, emotionally, and spiritually. The child or child's family members' may share similar survivor stories from their family or culture.

Kimmel, E. (1998). Dreidels. In: E. Kimmel (Ed.), *A Hanukkah treasury.* New York: Henry Holt and Company.

Procedure:
The therapist may begin the discussion by giving a brief summary of the client's movement from maltreatment to being a survivor. Key people, choices and use of resources should be noted. The therapist may then discuss survival from abuse or individuals or groups. The therapist may read one of the stories suggested above. The therapist and child discuss how survivors used clever methods and every day materials to escape from maltreatment. Across all types of abuse, survivors use coping skills. The similarities are noted.

Clients use art materials to create their path to freedom on a Survivor's Quilt. Paper, material or foam may be used as the base. Pieces of paper, foam or material may be glued to the base just as material pieces may be sewn together. In the original quilt, pieces of material representing rivers, fields, houses, and different types of crops were sewn together to show the path to freedom. On the Survivor's Quilt, the client may represent the steps on his or her journey. Their Survivor's Quilt may include a path, as a concrete representation of his or her movement from an abusive home to the current safe environment, or a symbolic representation. The quilt can include representations of people who have assisted his or her on his or her path from abuse to safety. The quilt may also include places such as foster homes, the court house, or social services that have been important on their journeys to safety. The quilt may include symbols of coping skills (i.e., clouds representing imagery). It may also include common items that may have provided safety or purpose in the face of adversity. For example, a child who read to escape, even temporarily, the reality of an abusive home, may include a picture of a book on his or her quilt. The quilt is taken home as a transitional object and reminder of his or her journey.

Name of activity: Pop Goes the Weasel: The Jack-in-the-Box as a Metaphor for Intrusive Thoughts and Demonstration of Anxiety Reduction with Exposure

Treatment Theme: Interventions for Processing Trauma

Recommended Age Range: 4 to 12 years

Treatment Modality: Individual

Goals:
1. Provide psychoeducation about intrusive thoughts.
2. Provide an opportunity for empowerment by seeing that fear and anxiety can lessen when repeatedly facing the fear (in vivo exposure).

Materials: A Jack-in-the-Box

Cost of Intervention: $$

Advance Preparation: None needed.

Discussion:

In vivo exposure to innocuous stimuli is an important component of effective treatment of anxiety. Exposure allows the child to become less anxious about the stimuli through the experience of tolerating fear. Once coping skills are developed, children who have been traumatized benefit from exposure to innocuous cues associated with the trauma. Gradual exposure techniques have been included as an important component of trauma treatment since initial use by Deblinger and Heflin (1996). An example of in vivo exposure may be a child who was sexually abused who has associated his or her bedroom with abuse. The bedroom, which is innocuous, is feared while in reality it is an innocuous stimulus. If the child is appropriately exposed to the stimuli, in this case his or her bedroom, he or she can overcome fear. It is important to note that exposure should only be done when it is known that the stimuli is innocuous (Cohen, Mannarino, & Deblinger, 2006).

Cohen, Mannarino, and Deblinger (2006) have noted that exposure should only be done when the parent is supportive of it. However, it is also important for the child or adolescent to have information about the process. This intervention allows for a playful and child-friendly method of introducing the concept of in vivo exposure and how exposure can decrease fear. As the child plays with the Jack-in-the-Box, he or she has a lessened response to the character popping out. This can be described to the child; however, a verbal description is likely not sufficient. Children often have heard of Jack-in-the-Boxes; however, most have not played with them. The Jack-in-the-Box allows for physical manipulation and a different level of understanding of the metaphor of a Jack-in-the-Box.

The clinician should use clinical judgment to determine whether the child's level of anxiety would respond well to this intervention. If the Jack-in-the-Box would result in the child being scared enough to avoid the toy instead of facing it and seeing joy in overcoming their anxiety, this intervention should not be used.

Cohen, J., Mannarino, A., & Deblinger, E. (2006). *Treating trauma and traumatic grief in children and adolescents.* New York: Guilford Press.

Deblinger, E. & Heflin, A.H. (1996). *Treating sexually abused children and their nonoffending parents: A cognitive behavior approach.* Thousand Oaks, CA: Sage.

Procedure:

The Jack-in-the Box is presented to the child and the child plays with it. After the child has experienced the character popping out several times, the clinician talks about how it may have been scary when the character in the Jack-in-the-Box first pops out but it becomes less scary as he or she did it repeatedly. This is compared to intrusive thoughts. The clinician and child discuss intrusive thoughts that the child has had or innocuous stimuli. The Jack-in-the-Box allows the child to have a slightly anxious response. Most children will jump and then laugh after seeing the Jack-in-the-Box pop out. They typically repeat this over and over to see the character pop out. After this repetition, many children articulate understanding that the repetition helped reduce their fear.

The clinician then discusses how exposure reduces anxiety. The Jack-in-the-Box acts as an example of how he or she can learn to control his or her anxiety by repeatedly facing the fear and "talking to themselves" about how he or she is going to respond. The Jack-in-the-Box play is followed by talking about how he or she is anxious at times related to intrusive thoughts or innocuous stimuli. The clinician discusses how the child can overcome his or her anxiety as they did with the Jack-in-the-Box.

The Jack-in-the-Box technique is followed by a discussion about a stimulus (one that is moderately distressing, so that the child's exposure allows for feelings of mastery) that the child could be exposed to and how the child can also decrease fear to that stimulus. The metaphor is discussed as needed during exposure to innocuous stimuli exposure to which the child is showing anxiety.

This intervention will also be published in: Cavett, A.M. (2011). The jack-in-the-box as metaphor for intrusive thoughts and to demonstrate anxiety reduction with exposure. In: Lowenstein, L. (Ed.), *Assessment and treatment activities for children, adolescents, and families. Volume 3: Practitioners share their most effective techniques.* Toronto: Champion Press

Safety

Planning

and

Termination

Title: My Safety Net

Treatment Theme: Safety Planning and Termination

Treatment Goals:
1. Assist the child in developing a support system.
2. Provide the child with information (appropriate to the support person's role) about how to contact members of his or her support system.

Treatment Modalities: Individual

Recommended Age Range: 4-12 years

Materials:
A nylon net for stuffed animals
Yarn
Small pieces of cloth
Scissors

Cost of Intervention: $ (Dependent upon whether parents supply the nylon net)

Discussion:
The support system of the child, comprised of family members, community supports, members of the child's faith community, and leaders of extracurricular activities, are beneficial to children. When a child is in therapy, the support system can be directly and indirectly involved in making changes in the child's life and helping the child make progress towards therapeutic goals. The safety net is a metaphor for protection and a tool to catch someone when he or she falls. This intervention is an activity to make discussing the support system (those people who catch the child when needed) more engaging. The net itself acts as a reminder of the abstract concept. Throughout treatment, the child's support system is important to the therapeutic process. The child who is in the early stages of therapy can be encouraged to use the support system to provide support in meeting therapeutic goals. At termination, the support system is important to continue progress towards treatment goals and support continued emotional growth. For traumatized children, the support system is essential.

Procedure:
The child and therapist discuss the people the child has available for guidance and support. The safety net is discussed as a precautionary aid used to make sure someone who is elevated, such as a tight-rope walker, is protected if they fall. The metaphor is used to describe those people who are in the child's support system. Each person's name is written on a small piece of cloth with contact information that is appropriate for the relationship. The pieces of cloth are tied to his or her safety net. The child may also list coping skills that can be used to protect him or herself. The transitional object of the safety net can be taken home by the child and used to store stuffed animals which also represent comfort.

Title: Light My Path

Treatment Theme: Safety Planning and Termination

Treatment Goals:
1. Assist the child in identifying a support system with information (appropriate to the support person's role) about how to contact members of the support system.
2. Use a concrete example to represent the concept of giving support and "lighting someone's path".
3. Reinforce the individuals in the support system in their roles in the child's life.

Treatment Modalities: Individual/Family

Recommended Age Range: 4-18 years

Materials:
Flashlights
Paper lanterns (Available at Discount School Supplies)
Writing utensils such as markers
Foam or other art supplies to decorate the lanterns

Cost of Intervention: $

Discussion:
The child or adolescent's treatment often depends, at least to some degree, on his or her support system. The support system may consist of parents, extended family, teachers, principal, special education staff, social workers, community agencies, faith communities and extracurricular events staff such as coaches, Girl or Boy Scout leaders, or band directors. This intervention is to empower the child in identifying and using the support system. A therapist may help the child or adolescent list several people who "light my path." However as with other therapeutic concepts, children and adolescents may use the concept more if the client experiences it in lieu of just talking about it. Therefore, this intervention allows the child to experience the concept of his or her support group lighting his or her path. This intervention also allows the members of the child's support system to be reinforced in their roles.

Procedure:
The child begins by thinking of the people supportive in his or her life. Each person's name in the support group is written on a paper lantern. On each lantern, the child or adolescent writes or draws some of the things that the support person provides for him or her.

The path taken during therapy is discussed. At the beginning of therapy there were certain problems or challenges, the child is told. Therapy has been like a path with the goals of therapy being met along the way. The therapist notes that the child has gone from one point to another through the process of therapy and that the support system has assisted in the process. The therapist states that the path is like going from one point in the office to another. The child then lines the lanterns along his or her path.

At times, it may be beneficial for the members of the support group to attend a session after the lanterns are completed with a ceremony to recognize the child's progress and the support of each member of the support group. The child stands with the therapist at the beginning of the "path" along which each of the lanterns representing the supportive people and the respective people are lined. The child walks the path and stops at each person, giving the lantern to the support person and saying something about what that person has done to support him or her. The support person tells a short story or description of an area of the child's growth. The therapist may wish to briefly discuss what each support person will say to the child prior to the session. The child proceeds through the path from beginning to end. When finished, the members of the support group are given the lanterns as reminders of their role in supporting the child.

The Light My Path intervention allows the child to see who he/she has for support. Furthermore, this intervention is also beneficial for those who are supportive of the child. The members of the support system are reinforced from the acknowledgement of their important role in the child's or adolescent's therapy.

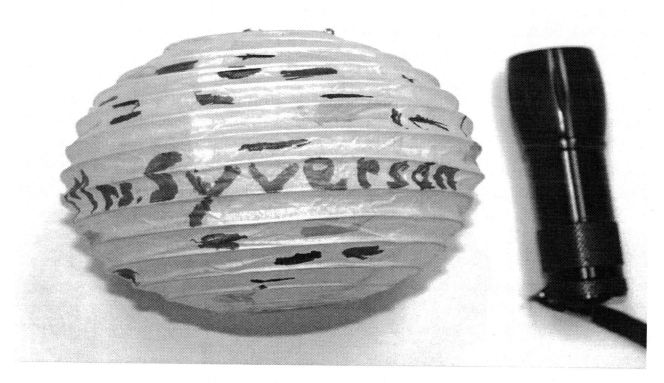

Figure 1: The paper lantern with a supportive person represented on it. The person's name may be written, or the lantern may be decorated to represent the relationship between the supportive person and the child. The flashlight to the right of the lantern is placed inside the lantern and placed alongside a path of lanterns.

Title: My Support Contacts and 411

Treatment Theme: Safety Planning and Termination

Treatment Goals:
1. Assist the child in developing a list of people who are emotionally supportive.
2. Provide the child with information about how to contact members of the support system.

Treatment Modalities: Individual/Family/Group

Recommended Age Range: 4-8 years

Materials:
Paper or cardstock
Markers/Colored pencils
Cell phone template
Scenarios following My Safe Neighborhood intervention

Cost of Intervention: $

Discussion:
Supportive communities are foundational for children. This intervention is a playful way to discuss the people in the child's life who provide support, and what type of support each provides. Children tend to want access to technology and electronics that they may see as giving them access to others and independence. For younger children, especially those who do not have a cellular phone, this desire can have a strong therapeutic benefit when processing how to access their community supports. This intervention allows the child to imagine that they have a cellular phone and that their contacts include those people who are the most supportive of them.

Procedure:
The child and therapist discuss how children need to have people available to them to make sure their needs are met, make sure they are safe, and provide love, nurturing, and relationship. The child is told that they can make a pretend cell phone that they can take with them after the session. The cell phone is drawn by the child or copied on cardstock from the outline provided. The child uses markers, crayons, or colored pencils to decorate the cell phone. As the child creates the cell phone, the therapist asks the child to list those people who make him or her feel the most safe and secure. They discuss a contact list and how a cell phone allows one to push a button for each person on the contact list. The therapist notes the importance of having supportive people so easily accessible.

The contact list, on their pretend cell phone, is created with the names and phone numbers of the child's supports. The therapist and child discuss who the child can go to for protection during certain situations. The therapist uses the scenarios provided following the My Safe Neighborhood intervention to role play common safety concerns. Puppets may be used during this role playing. During play, the child and therapist react to safety concerns to determine who would be the most appropriate person to contact about the problem. The therapist assists the child in adding the appropriate people to the contact list in the child's pretend cell phone.

The child can make a symbol by those who should be contacted under certain emergency or safety concerns. These are considered the Emergency contacts. Emergency numbers such as the police are also added. The phone number 4-1-1 is discussed as the number to call for getting information. The child is asked to make a symbol for people from whom he or she can get information. The child decides on the symbol with suggestions, such as the numbers 411 or a question mark, as needed. That symbol is drawn beside the supportive people who provide the child with information.

The parents and therapist can talk before the activity is utilized to gain their support and acquire the appropriate phone numbers to be used for the activity. The child is asked to talk with the parent at the end of the session.

Figure 1: Example of a cell phone drawing on which the child may write his or her emergency contacts and those from whom he or she can get the 4-1-1 (information).

Title: My Safe Neighborhood

Treatment Theme: Safety Planning and Termination

Recommended Age Range: 2 1/2-10 years

Treatment Goals:
1. Assist the child in identifying people who can be helpful in specific situations.
2. Playfully address safety planning.
3. Act out safety behaviors (actively seeking out helpers and asking for help).

Treatment Modalities: Individual/Family

Materials:
Toy cars including emergency vehicles
Children's rug with a village on it (Optional)
Toy village buildings and people (Optional)

Cost of Intervention: $

Discussion:
Safety planning is essential for children who come to therapy for trauma. Often safety planning is addressed with bibliotherapy or activities such as handouts. Although bibliotherapy and handouts can be helpful for reinforcing the concepts, it is often more engaging for children to play out the activities. This behavioral rehearsal makes the behaviors required to stay safe, more memorable. My Safe Neighborhood allows the child to play out several scenarios, practicing the steps required to stay safe in different situations.

In conjunction with the role playing and acting out of different safety situations, making plans with the family is important. The child and family should be aware of possible situations that may be dangerous. The child and family can discuss who an emergency contact is for the child. The family may come up with a secret word or code word to have someone use if they are picking the child up without the parent. The family can discuss and plan out safety plans for fires. This can be drawn on a map of the home. The place where everyone will meet after evacuating the home can be agreed upon. A list of emergency phone numbers can be made. The list from earlier interventions such as the Safety Net can be used to assist in developing an emergency phone list. The family may discuss what to do with pets in different emergencies. The family should be encouraged to keep their plans updated. The therapist can communicate with the family about what safety plans have been discussed prior to the My Safe Community intervention. The plans made prior to utilizing this playful intervention can inform and be consistent with the family's plans. The disasters or possible problems that the family may encounter but has not planned for can be discussed and the family can be assigned homework related to creating those plans. A disaster supply kit can be created by the family. A list of the items in the kit can be discussed. These may include nonperishable food, water, blankets, flashlights, batteries, medication, keys, money, identification, maps and warm clothing.

During the discussion, it is important to give accurate information and advice. For example, if a child indicates that they would return to the house to rescue a pet if there were a fire, it must be emphasized that he or she must not reenter a house when there is a fire. The importance of firefighters rescuing people and animals must be emphasized.

Children often feel safer when they know there is a plan for different emergencies. At times, children may respond with heightened anxiety to discussion about emergencies. The child's likely response should be discussed with the caregivers and considered prior to utilizing the intervention. Children who have been abused often need a clear message that adults will protect them from harm. Utilizing the My Safe Community intervention processes this concept with the child in a playful manner.

Procedure:

The child is engaged in pretend play and the therapist indicates that they are going to pretend to have a safe village and will talk about what to do to stay safe. Help the child identify several people who make his or her life safer including parents, grandparents, aunts, uncles, step or foster parents, and community members such as the police, firefighters, teachers, school counselors, psychologists, and doctors. The supportive people are represented by toys such as a doll. A toy such as a doll house is found for that person to "live" in the play. Toy police departments with police and a doctor in a toy clinic are represented. If the therapist has these play buildings, they can be utilized. If not, the child and therapist can find places in the office that represent the different buildings. For example, a small box may house the police department and a sheet of paper can represent the clinic or classroom. The respective vehicles are placed near the supportive toy people's buildings. Having a place for each of the supportive people can be done before or during the time that scenarios are introduced.

The following role-play scenarios are brought up in a playful manner and the child and therapist talk about who the child would talk to, whom would come to his or her aid and what things he or she might do to increase safety. Additional scenarios can be added to those the child has experienced and those which may exist again in the future.

Sample Safety Scenarios for My Support Contacts and My Safe Neighborhood

Sexual Abuse/Boundary Issues:

Abigail learned that the space around her is her "personal bubble" and that others can only go in it if she wants them to and feels comfortable. If her brother comes in when she is dressing and she feels uncomfortable, to whom can she go? What can she say? What if he keeps doing it? How does she know if it is okay or not? If you were in this situation, whom would you go to? How would you contact them?

Sara had an icky feeling about how her uncle hugged her. Whom could she go to, to talk about her feelings? Who will make sure she is safe? What can she do to help make sure she is safe? If you were in this situation, whom would you go to? How would you contact them?

Physical Illness:

Ashley doesn't feel good at school. Her tummy hurts and she feels like she might throw up. Whom can she talk to? What do you think they will do? Whom do you think they might call? What do you think will happen?

Keisha was jumping from the swings with her friends. Who might tell her whether this is safe? What could she do if she falls and thinks she has broken her leg?

What is the name of your doctor? Do you know your doctor's phone number? Who would contact the doctor if you needed it?

Physical abuse:

Joe's mom gets frustrated with him when he doesn't listen. Lately, she has spanked him. One time she slapped him. (Use discretion when deciding on the level of physical abuse represented. A level similar to what the client has previously experienced may be most helpful and least likely to be detrimental to the client.) Whom might he talk to? What do you think could happen to make sure he is safe? If you were in this situation, whom would you want to talk to?

Flooding:

Ethan hears the weather forecaster on the radio say that it has been raining heavily and more is on the way. A flood may be possible. Ethan and his parents start to take things upstairs from the basement. He wants to go to his friend's house, but his parents tell him he cannot go. What might he do? Where is he the safest? If water gets into his house and his toys are in the water, can he play with them again? (Everything that has been in flood water is contaminated. He should check with his parents about whether it can be disinfected. Otherwise it has to be replaced.) If there is just a little water in the streets, can he play in it? (No. Floods can be very quick. Stay away from the water.)

Tornado:

Brianna came home from school and needed to be home for an hour before her mom would be home from work. It is starting to rain and she heard on the TV that there is a chance of a tornado. What should she do? Whom might she talk to? Where would you go if there were a tornado? Whom would you talk to about your safety?

Fire:

Alexus woke up when she heard the fire alarm. Where should she and her family go? What might her mom or dad do to get help? What should she do if she left her electronics (or insert toy that the child would highly prize) inside? Who will come to the scene? Who will call the fire department?

Jamal's friend finds matches. He shows them to Jamal and wants to try them out to see if they can burn a candle in his mom's living room. What should Jamal do? (Tell an adult. Do not use the matches with his friend.)

Sandy smells fire and hears her mom say to get out of the house. How should Sandy get out? (She should crawl on her hands and knees.) Once she is out, she wants to go back in. How does she know when she can go back in the house? (When a firefighter tells her she can go back inside the building.)

What is the phone number for the fire station in your town? When would you call them? Do you have a safety plan with your parents/caregivers? How would you get out of the house? What is your route? Where would you meet once you got out of the house? Would you go back in to rescue your pet? (Stress to the child, not to go back into a burning house.) How often do your parents check your fire alarms? How do you move through a house if there is a fire? (Move on hands and knees.) If you get to a door, what should you do? (Only open a door if it is not hot.)

Domestic violence:

Sojourner's parents begin to argue. She feels scared and upset when she hears them. (Use discretion and describe a level of domestic violence that is similar to the experiences of the client) Sojourner hears her mom cry. She hears her parents yell at each other. She hears crashes and thinks things may be broken. She wonders whether her father/mother has hurt her mother/father. What might Sojourner do? Whom could she tell? What might happen if she talks to her father? Her mother? Whom would you talk to if your parents were fighting?

Bullying:

Bailey has several girls in her class who call her names. Lately, the girls have turned away from her when she walks towards them. Once she was pushed by one of the girls when the girl didn't want Bailey to sit where she was seated at lunch. What might Bailey do? Whom could she tell? What if the first person she tells does not do anything? What should she do if she is told to ignore it, and she tries that, but the girls continue to bully her?

Name of activity: Putting the Puzzle Pieces of Resiliency Together

Treatment Theme: Safety Planning and Termination

Recommended Age Range: 12 to 18 years

Treatment Modality: Individual/Family/Group

Goals:
1. Provide a concrete representation of change in therapy.
2. Provide a transitional object for the client at the time of termination.
3. Discuss resiliency factors/positive coping skills.

Materials:
Blank puzzles (Available at Discount School Supply)
Pencils, Crayons, Markers, Colored pencils

Cost of Intervention: $

Advance Preparation: None needed.

Discussion:

Putting the Puzzle Pieces of Resiliency Together is an intervention for older children and adolescents capable of abstract thought. When an adolescent initiates therapy, he or she may discuss his or her symptomotology in terms of a negative change in an abstract concept. For example, an adolescent who has been abused may feel a decrease in hope for the future. Some concepts likely have changed during the course of treatment. A child who has been abused may have come to therapy feeling his or her innocence was shattered, but throughout therapy may experience positive changes as well. The client may write "innocence" on the front (pre-therapy side) and "wisdom" on the back along with the things that helped the concept develop. This intervention can be helpful later in therapy after some of the shifts have occurred. If the client has not been able to make cognitive shifts to become more hopeful, develop positive relationships or learn to trust, then this intervention should be used later in treatment.

Description:

During a session in the termination phase, the client picks an abstract concept that seems to summarize many of original symptoms. The client can discuss what has facilitated change during therapy. For example, if the client chose HOPE, he or she may list things that have contributed to his or her increased hope. On the back of the puzzle the client can list those things (Developing a Relationship with Aunt Tesha, Teacher who believes in me, Faith in a spiritual belief) that allowed restoration in the belief (i.e., HOPE). Once the puzzle is finished, the client can take it apart (break HOPE) and put it back together with the changes/strengths/resiliency factors facing up. He or she will see a visual of his or her therapy process. The puzzle may act as a transitional object for the client when he or she leaving therapy.

Front of Puzzle: Word representing therapy such as HOPE.

HOPE

Back of Puzzle: Positive changes, strengths, or resiliency factors.

Knowing I can depend on Aunt Tesha.

Seeing that I can come out of pain and feel better again—things can get better.

Having friends (Jenn, NeeNee, Holly) whom I can rely on.

Previously published in: Cavett, A.M. (2010). Putting the puzzle pieces of resiliency together. In: Lowenstein, L. (Ed.), *Assessment and treatment activities for children, adolescents, and families. Volume 2: Practitioners share their most effective techniques*. Toronto: Champion

References and Suggested Resources

Adams, M. & Adams, J. (1991). Life events, depression, and perceived problem solving alternatives in adolescents. *Journal of Child Psychology and Psychiatry*, 32, 811-820.

Canino, I.A. & Spurlock, J. (1994). *Culturally diverse children and adolescents: Assessment, diagnosis, and treatment.* New York: Guilford Press.

Carle, E. (1997). *From Head to Toe Game.* Northampton, MA: Eric Carle Studio.

Cavett, A.M. (2010). Anger Menu. In: Lowenstein, L. (Ed.), *Assessment and treatment activities for children, adolescents, and families. Volume 2: Practitioners share their most effective techniques.* Toronto: Champion Press.

Cavett, A.M. (2009) *Playful trauma focused-cognitive behavioral therapy with traumatized children.* www.lianalowenstein.com/cavett.doc

Cavett, A.M. (2009). Playful trauma focused-cognitive behavioral therapy with maltreated children and adolescents. *Play Therapy* 4(3), 20-22.

Cavett, A.M. (2010). Putting the puzzle pieces of resiliency together. In: Lowenstein, L. (Ed.), *Assessment and treatment activities for children, adolescents, and families. Volume 2: Practitioners share their most effective techniques.* Toronto: Champion Press.

Cavett, A. M. (2010). Family strength genogram. In: Lowenstein, L. (Ed.), *Creative family therapy techniques: Play, art, and expressive activities to engage children in family sessions.* Toronto: Champion Press.

Cavett, A. M. (2010). Our family life scavenger hunt. In: Lowenstein, L. (Ed.), *Creative family therapy techniques: Play, art, and expressive activities to engage children in family sessions.* Toronto: Champion Press.

Cavett, A.M. (2011). The jack-in-the-box as metaphor for intrusive thoughts and to demonstrate anxiety reduction with exposure. In: Lowenstein, L. (Ed.), *Assessment and treatment activities for children, adolescents, and families. Volume 3: Practitioners share their most effective techniques.* Toronto: Champion Press.

Cohen, J., Mannarino, A., & Deblinger, E. (2006). *Treating trauma and traumatic grief in children and adolescents.* New York: The Guilford Press.

Crisci, G., Lay, M., & Lowenstein, L. (1998). *Paper dolls and paper airplanes: Therapeutic exercises for sexually traumatized children.* Indianapolis: Kidsrights.

Deblinger, E. & Heflin, A.H. (1996). *Treating sexually abused children and their nonoffending parents: A cognitive behavioral approach.* Thousand Oaks, CA: Sage.

DiTerlizzi, T. (2002). *The spider and the fly.* New York: Simon & Schuster Books.

Gil, E. (1991). *The healing powers of play: Working with abused children.* New York: Guildford Press.

Gil, E. (2006). *Helping Abused and Traumatized Children: Integrating directive and nondirective approaches.* New York: Guilford Press.

Grotsky, L, Camerer, C., & Damiano, L. (2000). *Group work with sexually abused children.* Thousand Oaks, CA: Sage Publications, Inc.

Goodyear-Brown, P. (2002). *Digging for buried treasure: 52 Prop-based play therapy interventions for treating the problems of childhood.* Nashville: Paris Goodyear-Brown.

Goodyear-Brown, P. (2005). *Digging for buried treasure 2: Another 52 Prop-based play therapy interventions for treating the problems of childhood.* Nashville: Paris Goodyear-Brown.

Gunarantana, B.H. (2002). *Mindfulness in plain English.* Somerville, MA: Wisdom Publications.

Hayes, S. C., Strosahl, K.D., & Wilson, K.G. (1999). *Acceptance and commitment therapy: An experiential therapy to behavior change.* New York: Guilford.

Hirshaw, S.P. & Erhardt, D. (1991). Attention-deficit hyperactivity disorder. In: P.C. Kendall (Ed.), *Child and adolescent behavior therapy: Cognitive-behavioral procedures* (pp. 98-130). New York: Guilford Press.

Hopkinson, D. (1993). *Sweet Clara and the freedom quilt.* New York: Dragonfly books.

Irwin, E.C. (2000). The use of a Puppet Interview to understand children. In: O'Connor, K.J. & Schaefer, C.E (Eds.), *Handbook of play therapy: Volume 2 Advances and innovations* (pp. 682-703). New York: John Wiley & Sons, Inc.

Kendall, P.C. (Ed.) *Child and adolescent therapy: Cognitive Behavioral Procedures (3rd Ed.).* New York: Guilford Press.

Kenney-Noziska, S. (2008). *Techniques, techniques, techniques: Play based activities for children, adolescents, and families.* West Conshohocken, PA: Infinity Publishing.

Kimmel, E. (1998). Dreidels. In: Eric Kimmel (Ed.), *A Hanukkah treasury.* New York: Henry Holt and Company.

Knell, S. (2000). Cognitive-behavioral play therapy In: O'Connor, K.J. & Schaefer, C.E. (Eds.), *Handbook of play therapy: Volume 2 Advances and innovations* (pp. 111-142). New York: John Wiley & Sons, Inc.

Knell, S. M. (1993). *Cognitive-behavioral play therapy*. Northvale, NJ: Jason Aronson.

Knell, S. (1994). Cognitive-Behavioral Play Therapy. In: O'Connor, K.J. & Schaefer, C.E (Eds.), *Handbook of play therapy: Volume 2 Advances and innovations* (pp. 111-142). New York: John Wiley & Sons, Inc.

Knell, S.M. & Beck, K.W. (2000). The Puppet Sentence Completion Task. In: K.J. O'Connor & C.E. Schaefer (Eds.), *Handbook of play therapy: Volume 2 Advances and innovations* (pp. 704-721). New York: John Wiley & Sons, Inc.

Levine, E. (2007). *Henry's Freedom Box: A true story from the Underground Railroad*. New York: Scholastic Press.

Lite, L. (1996). *A boy and a bear*. Plantation, FL: Specialty Press, Inc.

Lowenstein, L. (1999). *Creative interventions for troubled children and adolescents*. Toronto, ON: Champion Press.

Lowenstein, L. (2002). *More creative interventions for troubled children and adolescents*. Toronto, ON: Champion Press.

Lowenstein, L. (2006). *Creative interventions for bereaved children*. Toronto, ON: Champion Press.

Lowenstein, L. (2006). *Creative interventions for children of divorce*. Toronto, ON: Champion Press.

Lowenstein. L. (Ed.). (2008). *Assessment and treatment activities for children, adolescents, and families: Practitioners share their most effective techniques*. Toronto, ON: Champion Press.

Lowenstein, L. (Ed.). (2010). *Creative family therapy techniques: Play, art, and expressive activities to engage children in family sessions*. Toronto: Champion Press.

Lowenstein, L. (Ed.). (2010). *Assessment and treatment activities for children, adolescents, and families. Volume 2: Practitioners share their most effective techniques*. Toronto: Champion Press.

Lowenstein, L. (Ed.). (2011). *Assessment and treatment activities for children, adolescents, and families. Volume 3: Practitioners share their most effective techniques*. Toronto: Champion Press.

McGoldrick, M., Gerson, R., & Petry, S. (2008). *Genograms: Assessment and intervention*. New York: W.W. Norton & Company.

Miller, P. (2002). *Theories of developmental psychology*. New York: Worth Publishers.

O'Conner, K. J. (1983). The Color Your Life Technique. In: C.E. Schaefer & K.J. O'Conner (Eds.), *Handbook of play therapy*. New York: John Wiley and Sons.

Saltzman, A., & Goldin, P. (2008). Mindfulness-based stress reduction for school-aged children. In: L.A. Greco, & S.C. Hayes (Eds.), *Acceptance and mindfulness treatment for children and adolescents: A practitioner's guide*. Oakland, CA: New Harbinger.

Schaefer, C. E. (1995). The therapeutic powers of play. Northvale, NJ: Jason Aronson.

Semple, R. J. & Lee, J. (2008). Treating anxiety with mindfulness: Mindfulness-based cognitive therapy for children. In: L.A. Greco & S. C. Hayes (Eds.), *Acceptance and mindfulness treatment for children and adolescents: A practitioner's guide*. Oakland, CA: New Harbinger

Shirk, S. & Harter, S. (1996). Treatment of low self-esteem. In: M. A. Reinecke, F. M. Dattillio, & A. Freeman (Eds.), *Cognitive Therapy with children and adolescents: A casebook for clinical practice*. New York: Guilford Press, Inc.

Stark, K.D., Hargrave, J., Sander, J., Custer, G., Schnoebelen, S., Simpson, J., & Molnar, J. (2006). Treatment of childhood depression: The ACTION treatment program. In: P.C. Kendall (Ed.), *Child and adolescent therapy: Cognitive behavioral procedures*. New York: Guilford Press.

Twohig, M.P., Field, C.E., Armstrong, A.B., & Dahl, A.L. (2010). Acceptance and mindfulness as mechanisms of change in mindfulness-based interventions for children and adolescents. In: R.A. Baer (Ed.), *Assessing mindfulness and acceptance processes in clients: Illuminating the theory and practice of change*. Oakland: New Harbinger Press.

Vygotsky, L.S. (1967). Play and its role in the mental development of the child. *Soviet Psychology, 17*, 66-72.

Woodbury, K.A., Roy, R., & Indik, J. (2008). Dialectical behavior therapy for adolescents with borderline features. In: L.A. Greco, & S.C. Hayes (Eds.), *Acceptance and mindfulness treatment for children and adolescents: A practitioner's guide*. Oakland, CA: New Harbinger.

Woodson, J. (2005). *Show way*. New York: G.P. Putnam's Sons.

Ziegler, D. (2002). *Traumatic experience and the brain: A handbook for understanding and treating those traumatized as children*. Phoenix: Acacia Publishing.

Web Resources

<u>**Play Therapy Associations**</u>:

Association for Play Therapy	www.a4pt.org
British Association for Play therapy	www.bapt.info
Canadian Play Therapy Association	www.cacpt.com
International Society for Child and Play Therapy	www.playtherapy.org

<u>**Play Therapists with Publications of Structured Play Therapy Interventions**</u>:

Angela M. Cavett, Ph.D., L.P., RPT-S	www.childpsychologicalservices.com
David Crenshaw, Ph.D., ABPP	www.playtherapytechniques.com
Paris Goodyear-Brown, MSSW, LCSW, RPT-S	www.parisandme.com
Sueann Kenney-Noziska, MSW, LISW, RPT-S	www.playtherapycorner.com
Liana Lowenstein, LSW, RSW, CPT-S	www.lianalowenstein.com

<u>**Mental Health Organizations**</u>:

American Art Therapy Association, Inc.	www.arthterapy.org
American Psychological Association	www.apa.org
American Red Cross	www.redcross.org
Association for Children's Mental Health	www.acmh-mi,org
National Association of Social Workers	www.socialworkers.org
National Child Traumatic Stress Network	www.nctsnet.org
National Institute for Mental Health	www.hhs.gov

Child Abuse Prevention and Treatment:

Child Abuse Prevention   www.preventchildabuse.org

Centers for Disease Control and Prevention (CDC)   www.cdc.gov

American Professional Society on the Abuse of Children   www.apsac.org

Childhelp   www.childhelp.org

Trauma Focused-Cognitive Behavioral Therapy (TF-CBT)
Brief TF-CBT training   www.tfcbt.musc.edu

Resources for
Play Therapy Toys and Props

Child Therapy Toys
3355 Bee Cave Road
Suit 610
Austin, Texas 78746
866-324-PLAY (Phone)

www.childtherapytoys.com

Childswork Childsplay
PO Box 1246
Wilkes-Barres, PA
18703-1246
800-962-1141 (Phone)

www.childswork.com

Constructive Play Things
13201 Arrington Road
Grandview, MO 64030
800-448-7830 (Phone)

www.constplay.com

Discount School Supply
P.O. Box 6013
Carol Stream, IL 60197-6013
800-627-2829 (Phone)
800-879-3753 (Fax)

www.discountschoolsupplies.com

Folkmanis Puppets
Folkmanis, Inc.
1219 Park Avenue
Emeryville, CA 94608
info@folkmanis.com

www.folkmanis.com

Learning Resources
380 N. Fairway Drive
Vernon Hills, IL 60061
800-222-3909 (U.S. and Canada) or 847-5738400 (US and International)

www.learningresources.com

Melissa and Doug
800-284-3948

www.MelissaAndDoug.com

Oriental Trading Company
P.O. Box 2308
Omaha, NE 68103-2308
(800) 228-2269

www.orientaltrading.com

Ron's Trays
(Formerly Oak Hill Specialties)
P.O. Box 152
Cloverdale, CA 95425
707-894-4856

www.sandtrays.com

Self Esteem Shop
32839 Woodward Ave
Royal Oak, MI 48073
248-549-9900, 1-800-251-8336 (Phone)
248-549-0442 (Fax)

www.selfesteemshop.com

Self Help Warehouse, Inc.
1720 Epps Bridge Pkwy
Suite 108-390
Athens, GA 30606

www.selfhelpwarehouse.com

Smethport Specialty Company
P.O. Box 263
Smethport, PA 16749

Toys of the Trade
838 E. High St., #289
Lexington, KY 40502.
866-461-2929 (859-225-0304) Phone
866-803-3781 (859-225-3852). Fax

www.toysofthetrade.com